TELL ME WHEN?

CHANCELLOR
❧ PRESS ❧

An Hachette UK Company
www.hachette.co.uk

First published in 2002 by Chancellor Press,
a division of Octopus Publishing Group Ltd
Carmelite House, 50 Victoria Embankment,
London EC4Y 0DZ
www.octopusbooks.co.uk

Paperback edition 2010
This edition published in 2014 by Chancellor Press,
a division of Octopus Publishing Group Ltd

ISBN: 978-0-7537-2806-2

A CIP catalogue record for this book is available from the British Library

Printed and bound in China

3 5 7 9 10 8 6 4

CONTENTS

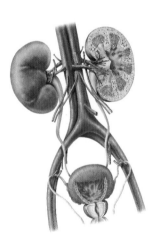

SCIENCE AND

TECHNOLOGY

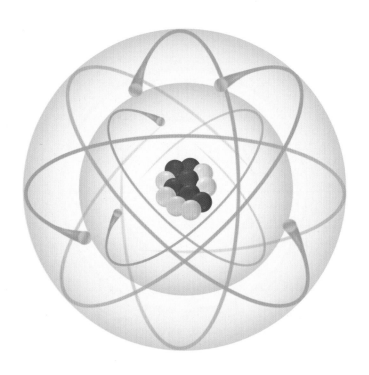

CONTENTS

· · · · · · · · · · · · · · · · · · · ·

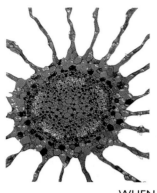

WHEN WAS THE FIRST PLASTIC MADE?

Plastics are made by a chemical process called polymerization. Nineteenth century chemists understood the making of plastics. The first plastic, vinyl chloride was made in 1838, closely followed by styrene in 1839, acrylics in 1843 and polyester in 1847. However, the vast potential for their use was not understood. Later that century, cheaper, substitute manufacturing materials were needed. In 1869, John Hyatt discovered celluloid when looking for a substitute for ivory. This revolutionary

A toy duck: a good example of how easily plastic can be moulded

material was tough and malleable; it started a wave of chemists developing new synthetic materials. In 1909, Leo Bakeland was responsible for the biggest development when he discovered phenolformaldehyde. This material was cheap to produce and could be moulded into any shape. He called it Bakelite and it was the first synthetic material to be mass-produced. The space technology of the late 1960s, among other developments, has been applied by scientists to develop new plastics and other synthetic materials. In the 21st century, we need to conserve our environment, so new biodegradable materials, are constantly being sought.

FACT FILE

Plastic is an ideal material for producing rainwear. It is water-resistant, air-permeable, shrink-resistant and can be easily wiped down.

WHEN WAS CLAY FIRST USED?

Clay is believed to have been used to make ceramic objects for at least 15,000 years. Certainly, fragments of clay pots have been found which date back to the Neolithic period, over 10,000 years ago.

As early as 5,000 years ago people learned how to make their clay pots stronger and watertight, using fire. People soon discovered that by burning clay, its properties changed completely.

The uses of clay broadened from making small vessels to building materials. Clay-based bricks and tiles were amongst the first composite materials. Egyptian wall paintings of 5,000 years ago show clay workers making such bricks and pots.

A traditional potter's wheel

The more adept at using clay people became, the more intricate the products they made. Some pottery which dates back thousands of years shows a high artistic quality in their production; examples of this are common from the Far East.

Through the ages, the use of clay in construction increased even more. Still today, ceramics is a huge industry world-wide.

FACT FILE

Ancient brick-makers fired bricks in kilns (special ovens) to produce building materials for structures that were intended to last.

WHEN WAS PAPER FIRST MADE?

The first paper was made about 2,000 years ago in China, by a man called Ts'ai Lun. He took the stringy inner bark of the Mulberry tree and pounded it in water until it became a mass of flattened threads. He then placed this pulped solution onto a flat tray of fine bamboo strips.

The water was allowed to drain through the bamboo, and the threads in the bamboo were left to dry. The dried result was a flat, fibrous material considered to be the very first paper.

FACT FILE

The Chinese had another secret, they were the only people who knew how to make silk. European traders would make the long journey to take silk back to Europe.

As with all new discoveries, improvements were gradually made. One of these was to brush starch over the paper to improve it.

The technique of making paper was taken to Russia and the Middle East by Chinese traders and from there it spread to Europe. Paper making was revolutionary in the spread of knowledge and mass production began. The first continuous paper-making machine was developed in France by Louis Robert in 1798. At the start of the nineteenth century, the Fourdrinier brothers developed the idea further in London. Nowadays we produce wood-free paper in an attempt to limit the damage to our environment.

WHEN WERE THE FIRST BOOKS MADE?

The *Diamond Sutta*, the oldest printed book known, made in CE 868

The first books were made about 4,000 years ago by the Egyptians who took flattened layers of papyrus stems to make sheets. The 'books' they made were collections of rolled papyrus sheets – very different from a book of today.

In the middle of the fifth century, parchment (sheep skin) replaced papyrus. Parchment sheets were placed on top of one another and bound down one side with leather thongs.

But it was in the Middle Ages that books as we know them today evolved. Vellum (calf skin) was made into sheets, and each piece was folded down the middle. Four vellum sheets made eight leaves and was considered a section. Unlike parchment, vellum was thick enough to be written on both sides. Finished sections were sewn together down the back fold (the spine) and covered with wooden boards front and back. The boards and spine were then covered with leather; the result was a book similar to that of today.

FACT FILE

In about CE 500 monks would spend endless hours on illuminated handwritten books. The work was slow and painstaking, but worthwhile because it was another way to show dedication to God.

WHEN DID GOLD MINING BEGIN?

Although the time cannot be pinpointed exactly, it is widely believed that gold mining extends back about 5,000 years. The first gold was mined in Egypt, which remained the centre of gold production until the first or second century CE. Egyptian wall paintings show gold mining in its various stages. In those days, gold was panned from water; this was achieved by sifting out the lighter sands in the water to leave the heavier, gold particles behind. By 3,000 BCE gold rings were used as a form of payment.

Panning for gold

With the exception of coins, gold was used only for decorative purposes.

Around 2,000 BCE mine shafts were constructed to obtain gold ore found in pockets deep in the ground; the Greeks and Romans became particularly adept at this.

FACT FILE

Gold standard was a monetary system in which the standard unit of currency is a fixed quantity of gold. It was first put into operation in Great Britain in 1821.

WHEN WERE STAINED GLASS WINDOWS INTRODUCED?

Ornate examples of stained glass in church windows

Historical documents and excavations have discovered that stained glass was around as far back as the 12th century. These are true stained glass windows which tell a pictorial story and are considered the invention of Western Europe.

Religious writings dating as far back as 240 CE mention the existence of tinted glass in windows of the early Christian basilicas.

Stained glass windows of medieval times were basic in their manufacture. The window opening was filled with thin sheets of marble or wood, with holes pierced through. Tinted glass was placed in the holes; this was known as a mosaic window. Leading was also used to join pieces of glass together to make attractive patterns in the windows.

FACT FILE

Circular turrets on medieval castles had very unusual windows – they were very narrow slits. Because they were built as fortresses the windows were designed to minimize the chance of being hit by arrows.

WHEN WAS THE FIRST AEROPLANE FLIGHT?

FACT FILE

Concorde is a supersonic airliner. The sonic 'boom' it produces, together with noise and air pollution concerns, has limited the development of such aircraft.

The first ever powered, sustained and controlled aeroplane flight took place at Kitty Hawk, North Carolina, USA, on December 17, 1903.

Orville Wright and his brother Wilbur both designed and built the plane for this historic flight. Orville piloted the first flight in the aircraft, aptly named the *Flyer*. He travelled 120 feet through the air in 12 seconds; Wilbur managed 175 feet in 12 seconds straight after this. They each had one more attempt: Orville flew 200 feet in 15 seconds, before Wilbur recorded the longest flight of the day, travelling 852 feet in 59 seconds.

The *Flyer*

WHEN WAS THE HOVERCRAFT INVENTED?

The hovercraft was invented in 1955 by the British scientist Christopher Cockerell. He decided to solve a problem that had been baffling scientists for 80 years. In the 1870s, the British engineer John Thornycroft began to design a ship that moved along on a cushion of air to reduce friction between the ship's hull and the water. He was unable to work out how to contain the cushion of air under the boat, but Cockerell solved this by attaching a rubber skirt to the bottom of the boat. This idea worked perfectly and the hovercraft was born.

FACT FILE

A boat is a pretty large object, yet it floats easily on the surface of water. This is because the fluid actually holds it up. The liquid offsets the force of gravity. If you want to feel this force, just take a blown-up beach ball into water. The water seems to push up the ball.

WHEN WERE NUCLEAR WEAPONS FIRST USED?

FACT FILE

In 1962 the Cuban crisis erupted when the USA discovered that the USSR was building missile sites on the island of Cuba in the Caribbean. The two superpowers came to the brink of war before the USSR agreed to withdraw the weapons.

Nuclear weapons were first used in 1945, at the end of World War II. Two bombs were dropped on the Japanese cities of Hiroshima and Nagasaki by the USA.

Hundreds of thousands of people were killed as a result of these two bombs, leaving a trail of destruction never seen in war before.

This was not only an important turning point in the war, but also a major turning point in history. Nuclear bombs became a new, deadly threat with huge, destructive consequences. The nuclear age had begun.

WHEN DID THE CHERNOBYL DISASTER OCCUR?

On 25-26th April, 1986 a serious accident occurred at the Chernobyl nuclear power station in the Ukraine. Some technicians in the power station attempted a poorly devised experiment. In doing this they shut down the reactor's safety system. The reactor continued to be powered, but in a dangerous state. The chain reaction in the core of the reactor led to a massive explosion, and radiation was emitted in huge quantities. Contaminated clouds carried the radiation not just over parts of Russia, but over the rest of the world.

FACT FILE

In the 1970s, organizations such as Friends of the Earth and Greenpeace began to campaign on many environmental issues. These included nuclear weapons, destruction of the rainforests, and dumping of toxic waste.

WHEN WAS FIRE DISCOVERED?

Fire has been known to man since the earliest times. Archaeologists have found evidence of charcoal and charred remains of bone amongst stones, dating back thousands of years.

It is likely that early man knew how to use fire before he understood how to create it. If, for example, lightning struck a tree and set it alight, man would have had the use of the fire and would have been able to keep it going.

Cavemen would have noticed sparks created when they trampled on loose stones. It is unlikely, though, that they would have immediately understood that the friction of two stones rubbing together created the sparks. It may have been generations before this idea was put into practice. Almost certainly the first fires that man experienced would have started by accident or as the result of nature, hence the lightning idea.

FACT FILE

Coke is a fuel produced by roasting coal in large 'coke ovens' at extremely high temperatures. In these ovens, there is not enough oxygen for the coal to burn; instead, it is roasted which removes gases and leaves the almost pure carbon called coke.

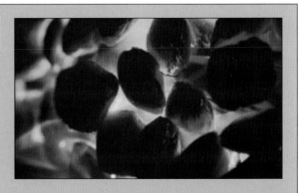

WHEN WERE MATCHES INVENTED?

The very first 'matches' were designed by early man when he had discovered fire. Rubbing two pieces of flint together to create a spark with which to ignite dry leaves is a basic fire-lighting creation.

Modern matches, like those pictured above, were made possible by the discovery of phosphorus, a substance which catches fire at a low temperature.

In the nineteenth century, various forms of 'matches' were designed using phosphorus. Often, strips of wood were tipped with white or yellow phosphorous. However white and yellow phosphorous is highly flammable, and dangerous to use.

The first safety matches were made in Sweden in 1844, with the introduction of non-poisonous red phosphorous. Instead of putting all the necessary chemicals for ignition on the match-head, the red phosphorous was painted onto the striking surface of the match box.

FACT FILE

Stone Age people made fire using a simple wooden stick called a fire drill. The drill was turned quickly over a piece of dry wood until it produced enough heat to start the fire.

WHEN WAS MORSE CODE DEVELOPED?

Morse code is a messaging system which uses two kinds of signal, a short one called a dot, and a long one called a dash. The signals are sent via telegraphs. A transmitter sends a coded message in long and short bursts of radio waves along a wire; the receiver then translates the dots and dashes into their representative letters, numbers and words.

Samuel Morse (1791-1872) was an American engineer who developed this system. He conceived the idea of some sort of communication via telegraph in 1832. After several years of work on the idea, Morse perfected it in 1838.

However, at that time, telegraph lines did not exist across land, so there was no way Morse could put his code to use on a practical scale.

It was 1843 before the US government allocated a sum of money to construct a telegraph line between Washington and Baltimore. Morse sent the first Morse Code message along the lines in 1844.

FACT FILE

Morse code was used a lot during World War I because it was a quick and easy way of sending messages. Probably the most famous signal was SOS which actually stood for 'Save our Souls'.

S • • •

O – – –

S • • •

18

WHEN WAS BRAILLE INVENTED?

The Braille system was invented in 1829 by a blind gentleman called Louis Braille. He developed a system which would allow blind people to read and write. It is today one of the most widely used alphabets for the blind.

The Braille system consists of dots. Each letter of the alphabet is represented by a combination of dots. These combinations are punched onto paper, so that they appear as raised bumps. A blind person reads the dots by moving their fingers over the bumps, recognising each letter to spell out the words.

There were earlier systems of reading for the blind. Even as far back as 1517, alphabetic letters were engraved onto blocks of wood for the blind to read. This system was good to read by, but the drawback was that the blind could not see how to form the letters when they wanted to write.

The sensitive tip of the finger 'feels' the Braille letters

FACT FILE

Semaphore is a means of communicating by using flags. Different flag positions represent different letters and numbers. It was widely used between ships sailing near each other in the days before radio.

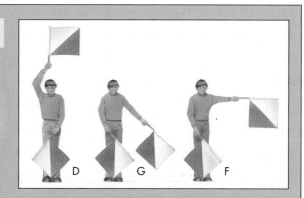

WHEN WAS THE TELEVISION INVENTED?

An early broadcast

The television was not 'invented' at one particular time by one particular person. The processes which enable a television to operate were developed over a period of time.

In 1875, G. R. Carey made the first basic television system using photoelectric cells. An object was focussed through a lens onto a bank of photoelectric cells. Each cell controlled how much electricity would be passed on to a light bulb. Crude outlines of the object then appeared in lights.

In 1923 the first practical transmission of pictures over wires was acieved. There was also a great development in television camera technology.

By 1945 the television as we know it today had been developed.

Twenty first century technology has brought high definition digital television and flat screen interactive television sets, with hundreds of satellite channels.

FACT FILE

With the use of communication satellites, TV programmes can be beamed to the most remote parts of the world, including the Amazon jungle!

WHEN WAS THE INTERNET STARTED?

The internet was created in 1983. The idea behind the internet came from the US Defence department who had a basic version of the internet set up as a secure system for their information.

The internet was born from a mainly academic origin, as a framework connecting numerous computer networks together. It has rapidly developed into a very popular commercial medium. By the mid-1990s, millions of computers all around the world were connected on the 'world wide web'.

The limits of technology are always changing, and the internet tests the capabilities of modern developments to the full.

FACT FILE

Modern communications have affected our lives in many ways. Since the 1980s the mobile phone has proved to be an increasingly popular means of communication. It was publicly introduced in Chicago in 1983 and was a success from the start.

WHEN WAS THE HEYDAY OF CANAL BUILDING?

A large commercial shipping canal

People have used canals to transport heavy goods for thousands of years. It is believed the first canals were built to join together existing rivers to make a transport route. Indeed, the city of Venice in Italy was built on a system of canals rather than roads; six thousand years ago the Aztec city of Tenochitlan was built with an impressive system of canals within it for transport.

However, the heyday of canal building was much more recent. The industrial revolution was responsible for the upsurge in canal building. There was a huge need during this era for cheap and easy ways to transport goods from factories to ports. Horse-drawn canal boats and steam-powered canal boats were faster than carrying cargo by horse-drawn carts along the road.

FACT FILE

Locks are an essential feature of any canal which needs to gain or lose height. A lock has gates that can be closed to control the water level in a section of the canal. Water is let into or taken from the section, raising or lowering the vessel inside.

WHEN WAS THE FIRST METAL BRIDGE BUILT?

It was the industrial revolution which brought about the introduction of metal bridges. In the past, bridges were constructed of stone and timber, which were available in large quantities. Iron was used because it was much stronger than either wood or stone, and was, on the whole, less expensive to produce. Bridges made from timber or stone became fewer and fewer.

The first ever metal bridge was built in England in 1779. The Coalbrookdale Bridge, which spanned the River Severn, was designed by Thomas Pritchard and built by Andrew Darby. This

bridge, the first to be built solely of iron, spanned almost 100 feet across the river in an almost perfect semi-circular arrangement of cast-iron pieces.

FACT FILE

The drawbridge originated in medieval Europe as a defensive feature of castles and towns. It was operated by a counterweight and winch. In the late 19th century drawbridges began to be built specifically to aid navigation; the Tower Bridge, London, being a fine example.

WHEN DOES LIGHTNING STRIKE?

To understand exactly what lightning is, we must recall a fact we know about electricity. We know that things become electrically charged – either positively or negatively. A positive charge has a great attraction for a negative one. As the charges become greater, this attraction becomes stronger. A point is finally reached where the strain of being kept apart becomes too great for the charges. A discharge takes place to relieve the strain and make the two bodies electrically equal. This is exactly what happens in the case of lightning. This discharge follows the path which offers the least resistance. That is the reason why lightning often zigzags. Moist air is only a fair conductor of electricity which is why lightning often stops when it starts raining.

FACT FILE

The electrical nature of the nervous system was discovered after Italian scientist Galvani noticed how frogs' legs twitched when an electrical current was applied to the nerve.

WHEN WAS LIGHTNING FIRST UNDERSTOOD?

Ben Franklin (1706–1790) was an American with many talents. He was a printer, scientist and politician who played an important part in founding the United States.

He discovered the nature of lightning while flying a kite during a thunderstorm. Franklin noticed sparks jumping from a key tied to the end of the wet string. This could very easily have killed him, but it did not. He went on to invent the lightning conductor, a strip of copper that is run from the top of a building to the ground in order that lightning can earth itself safely.

Lightning is a significant weather hazard and occurs at an average rate of 50 to 100 discharges per second. Lightning rods and metallic conductors can be used to protect a structure by intercepting and diverting the lightning current into the ground as harmlessly as possible. When lightning is likely to occur, people are advised to stay indoors or in a car, away from open doors and windows and to avoid contact with any electrical appliances or plumbing that might be exposed to the outside environment.

FACT FILE

A lightning conductor is a metal rod that is placed so that it points upwards above the highest point of a tall building. If lightning does strike the building, it is the conductor, not the building itself, that the spark hits.

WHEN DO WE SEE THE SPECTRUM OF LIGHT?

Sir Isaac Newton

TELL ME WHEN : SCIENCE AND TECHNOLOGY

Sir Isaac Newton of Cambridge University in England, first uncovered the secrets of how light is divided up. We think of ordinary light as being 'white', but really light is a mixture of red, orange, yellow, green, blue and violet. When sunlight strikes the bevelled edge of a mirror, or the edge of a glass prism, or the surface of a soap bubble, we can see the different hues in light. What actually happens is that the white light is broken up into the different wave lengths that are seen by our eyes. These wave lengths form a band of parallel stripes, each hue grading into the one next to it. This band is called a 'spectrum'. In a spectrum the red line is always at one end and the blue and violet lines at the other.

FACT FILE

Sir Isaac Newton used his discoveries about light to build a new kind of telescope. It used a reflecting mirror instead of glass lenses to magnify images.

WHEN WAS THE FIRST ELECTRIC LAMP IN USE?

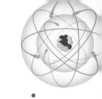

An early electric street light

An American inventor, Thomas A. Edison invented the first workable electric lamp in 1879. In the late 1800s electric lamps began to replace gas ones.

On October 21, 1879, Edison created a lamp containing a carbonized thread for the filament. The lamp burned steadily for two days.

The first commercial installation of Edison's lamp was made in May 1880 on the steamship Columbia. In 1881 a New York City factory was lit with Edison's system, and the commercial success of the incandescent lamp was quickly established.

FACT FILE

The tubes in modern low energy bulbs are full of mercury vapour and electronic ballast, through which electricity flows, The mercury vapour gives off light in the ultraviolet rang stimulating the phosphorous coating on the inside of the tubes to produce visible light.

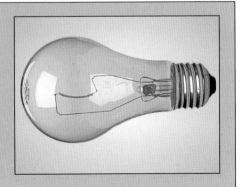

WHEN DID THE CANNING OF FOOD AND DRINK FIRST START?

People had been trying for thousands of years to find better ways to preserve food for a long time. The first patent for a 'tin canister' for preserving food was granted in England to Peter Durand in 1810. He got the idea from the canisters in which tea was packed. In America, the name became shortened to 'tin can', and the industry was called 'canning', while in England it is known as 'tinning'.

The first cannery in the United States was one for fish, and was started by Ezra Dagget in New York City in 1819. Heinz & Company began producing baked beans in tomato sauce at Richmond, Victoria on October 1, 1935. To can a food successfully, it must be heated enough to kill the organisms (moulds, yeasts, bacteria) that may cause fresh food to spoil; the tin can or glass jar must be free from germs and it must be sealed air-tight.

FACT FILE

In 1810 the French chef called Nicholas Appert discovered a way of preserving food by packing food into wide-mouth bottles. He sealed the bottles and then lowered them into a boiler filled with hot water. A lid was put on, so that the bottles would heat in their boiling water bath. Some foods, fruit and vegetables in particular, may also be preserved by pickling then stored in jars.

WHEN WAS YEAST FIRST USED IN BAKING?

Thousands of years ago, the Egyptians discovered that it was the yeast which made bread rise and so they were the first people to produce a 'yeast-raised' bread.

Yeast is a one-celled plant, so small that it cannot be seen without a microscope. As yeast plants grow and reproduce, they form two substances called 'enzymes', invertase and zymase. These enzymes help to change starch to sugar and sugar to alcohol, carbon dioxide and energy.

FACT FILE

The first bread was made in Neolithic times, nearly 12,000 years ago, probably of coarsely crushed grain mixed with water, with the resulting dough probably laid on heated stones and baked by covering with hot ashes.

This energy producing process is called 'fermentation'. The carbon dioxide formed is a gas which man may use in a number of ways; one of which is baking, particularly bread.

Modern breadmakers add yeast and sugar to the dough as they make it. The starch and sugar in the bread dough serve as food for the yeast. Carbon dioxide is given off and forms bubbles inside the loaf. Heat from the oven causes the gas to expand. This makes the bread rise even more. Finally, the heat drives off the carbon dioxide, and it leaves a light, dry loaf.

WHEN WERE FIREWORKS INTRODUCED?

Chinese crackers were probably the first fireworks to be made and this was about 2000 years ago. They are still used in China and throughout the East to celebrate weddings, births and religious festivals. They are also used to scare away evil spirits. It is probable that gunpowder was developed in China because they used potassium nitrate (saltpeter) to cure their meat, and so it was readily available.

Fireworks have also been used for centuries in ancient Indian and Siamese ceremonies.

The earliest recorded use of gunpowder in England is by the Franciscan monk Roger Bacon (born 1214). He recorded his experiments with a mixture which was very inadequate by today's standards but was recognisable as gunpowder. His formula contained charcoal and sulphur because there was no natural source of saltpeter available.

FACT FILE

In January 1606 Parliament in England established November 5 as a day of public thanksgiving. The day, known as Guy Fawkes Day, is still celebrated with bonfires, fireworks, and the carrying of 'guys' through the streets.

WHEN WAS GUNPOWDER FIRST USED?

It was the Chinese again who first started using gunpowder in warfare. By the year 1232, the Chinese had discovered black powder (gunpowder) and had learned to use it to make explosive bombs as well as propelling forces for rockets. Drawings made in military documents later show powder rockets tied to arrows and spears.

When the Mongols laid siege to the city of K'ai-feng, the capital of Honan province, the Chinese defenders used weapons that were described as 'arrows of flying fire'. In the same battle, it is reported, the defenders dropped from the walls of the city a kind of bomb described as 'heaven-shaking thunder'.

In the same century rockets appeared in Europe. There is indication that their first use was by the Mongols in the Battle of Legnica in 1241. The Arabs are also reported to have used rockets in 1249.

FACT FILE

Guy Fawkes is best known for his efforts to blow up the Parliament building in England, in 1605. This became known as the 'Gunpowder Plot'. His plan, however, was foiled and he was consequently arrested on 4 November, 1605.

WHEN DID RUTHERFORD FIRST SPLIT THE ATOM?

Ernest Rutherford (1871–1937) was a physicist who studied radioactivity. He found several different forms of radiation and also discovered that elements change as a result of radioactive decay. He received the Nobel Prize for his work. Rutherford went on to discover the nucleus of the atom, and in 1919 he finally succeeded in splitting an atom for the first time.

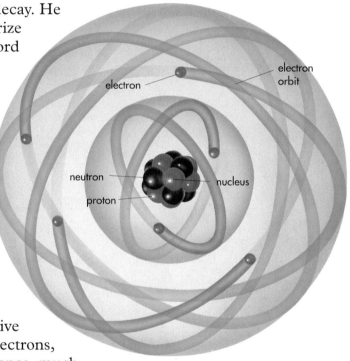

electron

electron orbit

neutron

proton

nucleus

He described the atom as a tiny, dense, positively charged core called a nucleus, in which nearly all the mass is concentrated, around which the light, negative constituents, called electrons, circulate at some distance, much like planets revolving around the Sun.

FACT FILE

Atoms become linked to other atoms by electrical bonds, which work rather like chemical hooks. Some atoms only carry one of these hooks while others may have many.

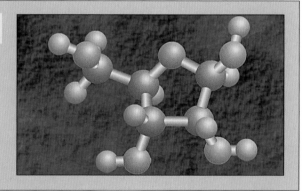

WHEN WAS ATOM STRUCTURE DISCOVERED?

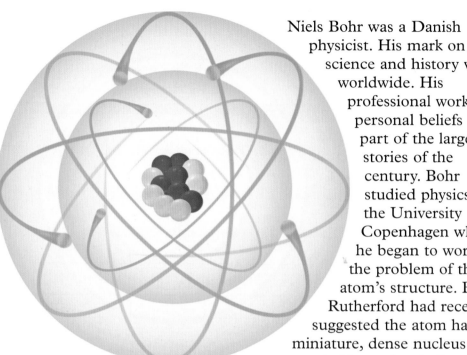

Niels Bohr was a Danish physicist. His mark on science and history was worldwide. His professional work and personal beliefs were part of the larger stories of the century. Bohr studied physics at the University of Copenhagen where he began to work on the problem of the atom's structure. Ernest Rutherford had recently suggested the atom had a miniature, dense nucleus surrounded by a cloud of nearly weightless electrons. There were a few problems with the model, however. Bohr proposed adding to the model and this proved to be a huge leap forward in making theory fit the experimental evidence that other physicists had found over the years. A few inaccuracies remained to be ironed out by others over the next few years, but his essential idea was proved correct.

He received the Nobel Prize for this work in 1922, and it is what he is most famous for. Bohr was only 37 at the time and went on to make many other discoveries.

FACT FILE

Niels Bohr helped to develop the atomic bomb in 1943.

WHEN WAS THE FIRST MICROSCOPE USED?

In the 16th century scientists were starting to look inwards at the secrets of the human body. They were able to use a new instrument to help them – the two-lens microscope which had been invented in about 1590.

The Dutchman Antonie van Leeuwenhoek (1632–1723) started by using ground glass lenses to examine the world about him.

In the 1670s he made his first crude microscope with a tiny lens and this allowed him to be the first person to see microscopic life such as bacteria, yeast and living blood cells. During his career, van Leeuwenhoek ground a total of 419 lenses, and his microscopes became progressively more effective.

The English scientist Robert Hooke used an early microscope, such as the one above, to discover the existence of living cells in plants.

FACT FILE

Some microscopes are so powerful they can magnify the smallest objects many thousands of times. This plant cell is invisible to the naked eye.

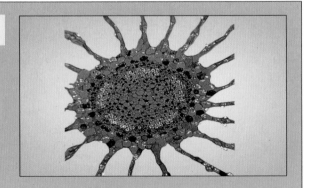

WHEN WAS THE TELESCOPE INVENTED?

Galileo is credited with having developed telescopes for astronomical observation in 1609. While the largest of his telescopes was only about 120 cm long and had an objective diameter of 5 cm, it was equipped with an eyepiece that provided an upright image. Galileo used his modest apparatus to explore the valleys and mountains of the Moon, the phases of Venus, and the four largest satellites, which had never been systematically observed before.

The reflecting telescope was developed in 1668 by Newton. He became the first person to use a telescope to see the moons orbiting the planet Jupiter. He also used his theories about gravity to show why the planets orbit the Sun.

FACT FILE

Special solar telescopes have been constructed so that the intensity of the image of the Sun or other planets, will not damage the observer's eye.

WHEN WAS THE CN TOWER BUILT?

The CN Tower in Toronto, Canada is a communications and observation tower. This building was completed in 1976, and at that time was the world's tallest free-standing structure.

The 20th century saw an explosion in communications technology. The first radio broadcast was made almost at the beginning of the century, when Reginald A. Fessenden transmitted music and words in 1906.

By the 1920s, radio provided a major form of entertainment for many people around the world. Then, in 1926, a Scottish engineer named John Logie Baird developed the first successful television set.

FACT FILE

Communication satellites are used to carry communications such as radio, television and telephone messages around the world. These satellites are 'parked' in an orbit where they will remain in position over the same part of the Earth's surface.

WHEN DO WE USE A MODEM?

Computers that are connected to a telephone line incorporate a device called a modem. It turns signals into a form that can be transmitted along the telephone line. The name 'modem' comes from the term Modulator-Demodulator. The device modulates, or changes, the digital signal from a computer into an analogue signal, which is the type of signal that travels along telephone lines. The modem decodes, or demodulates, the signals it receives back so they can be read by the computer. Some modems are 'voiceband'; that means they enable digital terminal equipment to communicate over telephone channels, which are designed around the narrow bandwidth requirements of the human voice.

FACT FILE

Robots, direct broadcast satellite, WiFi, and mobile phones all use modems to communicate, as do most other wireless services today.

THE

HUMAN BODY

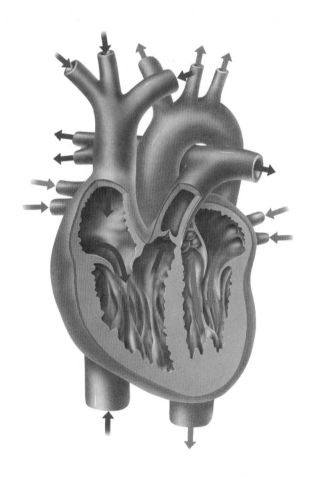

CONTENTS

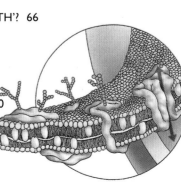

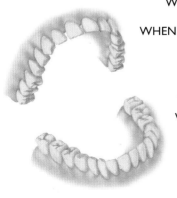

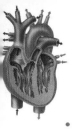

WHEN IS CONNECTIVE TISSUE NEEDED?

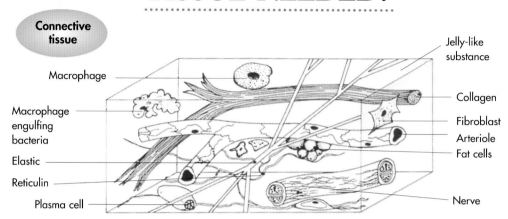

Connective tissue

Macrophage

Macrophage engulfing bacteria

Elastic

Reticulin

Plasma cell

Jelly-like substance

Collagen

Fibroblast

Arteriole

Fat cells

Nerve

The skeleton is the framework of our bodies which keeps the organs, blood vessels and nerves in place and also acts as protection. The connective tissue is needed to act as a support and to bind them all together. It also supplies the ligaments and tendons for the joints and muscles, tethers the larger organs to keep them in place, and provides softness for protection and rigidity in the form of cartilage.

There are many forms of connective tissue, but they are all developed from the same jelly-like substance which is made up of salts, water, protein and carbohydrate. Inside this jelly are elastic threads to give elasticity; collagen to give strength; reticulin to give support; white cells and macrophages to fight infection; fat cells for storage; and finally plasma cells to produce antibodies.

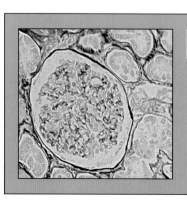

FACT FILE

The shape and appearance of a cell depends on what job it does. Cells consist of jelly-like cytoplasm, surrounded by a membrane. Nutrients pass through this membrane and substances produced by the cell leave.

WHEN ARE DIFFERENT JOINTS REQUIRED?

A joint is the meeting point between bones and usually controls the amount of movement. Some joints have to be strong, while others need to be very mobile. As it is not possible for joints to be both strong and mobile we require many different kinds of joints:

ELLIPSOID JOINT
Allows circular and bending movement but no rotation

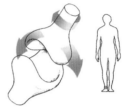

SADDLE JOINT
Allows movement in two directions, but without rotation

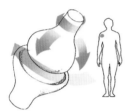

BALL-AND-SOCKET JOINT
A joint freely moving in all directions

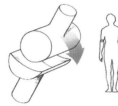

HINGE JOINT
Allows extension and flexion

CONDYLAR JOINT
This is similar to a hinge joint, but with slight rotation to allow the joint to 'lock' into an extended position

PIVOT JOINT
Allows rotation but no other movement

PLANE JOINT
A flat surface allows the bones to slide on each other, but they are restricted by ligaments to a small range

FACT FILE

The knee joint is the largest and most complex joint in the body. As it reaches full extension it rotates slightly and 'locks' into a rigid limb from hip to ankle.

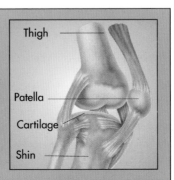

Thigh

Patella

Cartilage

Shin

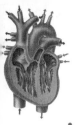

WHEN DO CELLS DIE?

All living things, plant and animal alike, are made from cells. An individual body cell is too small to be seen by the naked eye. Cells have a fixed lifespan and are replaced automatically as they die off. The more active the cell, the shorter the time it will live.

Some white blood cells live for a very short time, and some types that consume dead cells and bacteria survive for only about 30 hours.

White cells that fight disease live for two to four years. Cells lining the intestine live for about five days before being replaced.

Below is a list of the lifespan of certain cells:

- Skin cells live for 19 days
- Sperm live for 2 months
- Eyelashes live for 3 to 4 months
- Red blood cells live for 4 months
- Liver cells live for 8 months
- Scalp hairs live for 2 to 4 years
- Bone cells live for 15 to 25 years

A human body cell

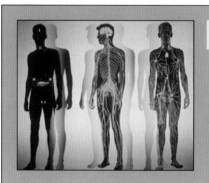

FACT FILE

There are three types of nerve cell each with a different function. Motor neurones control the way your muscles work. Sensory neurones carry messages from your sense organs. Connector neurones pass messages between different parts of the nervous system.

WHEN DOES THE BODY REPLACE DAMAGED CELLS?

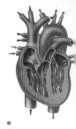

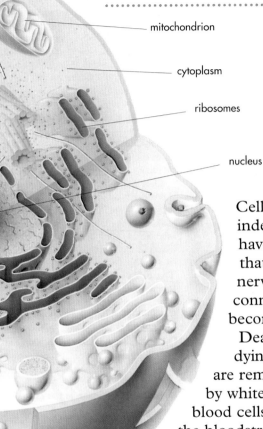

mitochondrion

cytoplasm

ribosomes

nucleus

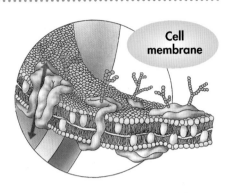

Cell membrane

Cells are able to divide very quickly indeed to replace those that are old or have died. Nerve cells are the only ones that cannot be replaced. However, even nerve cells can sometimes grow new connections if the message paths become damaged.

Dead and dying cells are removed by white blood cells in the bloodstream, which actually eat them. The liver is also able to break down red blood cells, which are only able to survive for a very short time. The cell's control area, the nucleus, contains all the information and instructions to keep the cells alive and functioning. The information the cell needs is in the form of immensely long coils of chemicals. These structures are known as DNA, which make up the genes.

FACT FILE

The largest cell in the human body is the egg cell or ovum, which may be fertilized by a sperm cell and grow into a baby.

WHEN IS A BABY'S GENETIC MAKE-UP DECIDED?

A baby's genetic make-up is fixed from the moment that the egg is fertilized. The division of the nucleus is an essential part of cell division. Each new nucleus contains two sets of genes: one provided by the mother, and the other by the father. Before the cell divides, both sets of genes are copied - termed DNA replication. Each new offspring then receives a full set of genes from each parent.

So it is that every human being inherits some of the characteristics of both parents. This why all kinds of traits, for example, height or curly hair run in families. However, every human being is also a unique individual, subject to the influences of the environment in which he or she grows, the food that is eaten and the illnesses that are caught. These circumstances affect emotional, intellectual and physical development too.

Scientists have debated the contribution that heredity and environment each make to the development of the individual. The Human Genome Project and the decoding of DNA suggest that heredity is more significant than was realized.

FACT FILE

A long thread or axon extends from the body of a neurone, and it is along this that the nerve impulses are carried.

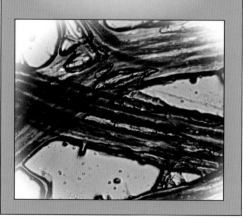

Mitosis – cell reproduction

WHEN DOES MITOSIS OCCUR?

As well as being packed with information, the DNA of chromosomes also has the ability to reproduce itself. Without this, the cells could not pass on information from one generation to the other. The process of cell division in which the cell duplicates itself is called mitosis, which works as follows:

1 the chromosomes become shorter and the nuclear envelope breaks,

2 the chromosomes are released, which duplicate and attach themselves to a cytoplasmic network,

3 they are then drawn apart

4–7 to form two new cells with reformed nuclear envelopes.

Mitosis is absolutely essential to life because it provides new cells for growth and for replacement of worn-out cells. Mitosis may take minutes or hours, depending upon the kind of cells and species of organisms. It is influenced by time of day, temperature, and chemicals. Strictly speaking the term mitosis is used to describe the duplication and distribution of chromosomes, the structures that carry our genetic information.

FACT FILE

DNA strands look like a twisted ladder. Sections of DNA are called genes. All the instructions for growing a new human being are coded into the DNA molecule.

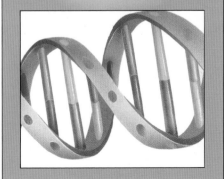

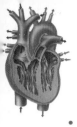

WHEN WERE GENES DISCOVERED?

In the 1800s a monk named Gregor Mendel experimented with characteristics in pea plants by cross-fertilizing plants with different traits. He kept a careful track of the traits displayed by the pea plants produced by cross-fertilization, discovering that the characteristics from the parent plants were inherited by the progeny (off-spring) plants in specific patterns.

Mendel also discovered during his experiments that certain genes seemed more dominant than others. For example, if a pea with a white flower is cross-fertilized with a pea with a pink flower, the resulting flowers will all be pink.

This is clear in human beings. A parent with brown-brown genes produces only children with brown eyes, while a parent with brown-blue genes could produce children with eyes other than brown.

Model of DNA

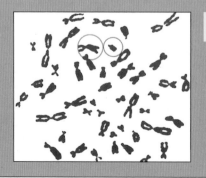

FACT FILE

Chromosomes are tiny threads that are present in all cells apart from red blood cells. They contain all the information for an entire person to develop. There are 46 chromosomes in each cell. They come in 22 pairs, plus another special pair that determine the person's sex.

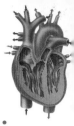

WHEN WAS HAEMOPHILIA DISCOVERED IN THE ROYAL LINE?

female carrier

male afflicted

female non-carrier

Edward Duke of Kent (1767–1820) · Victoria Princess of Saxe-Coburg (1786–1861)

possible female carrier

possible male afflicted

male unafflicted

Albert Prince of Saxe-Coburg-Gotha (1819–61) · Queen Victoria (1819–1901)

Leopold, Duke of Albany (1853–84) · Helen (1861–1922) · Louis IV (1837–92) · Alice (1843–78)

Edward VII, King of England (1841–1910) · Victoria Princess of Saxe-Coburg (1786–1861)

Victoria (1840–1901) · Frederick III Emperor of Germany (1831–88)

Beatrice (1857–1944) · Henry Prince of Battenburg (1858–96)

Haemophilia is an inherited deficiency whereby the substance necessary for blood clotting is missing. The transmission of this condition is sex linked, being present mostly in males but carried solely by females. Sons of a haemophilic male are normal, but daughters, although outwardly normal, may transmit this deficiency to half their sons.

The existence of haemophilia in certain royal families of Europe is well known. Working from family trees it seems probable that Queen Victoria naturally produced the gene for haemophilia.

FACT FILE

When we look at other human bodies, we usually concentrate on the face. Our features are largely inherited, under control of the genes, which is why we resemble our parents.

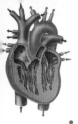

WHEN DO PEOPLE GET HEART ATTACKS?

Your heart is a powerful muscle which pumps blood around your body. It is only the size of your fist and weighs less than half a kilogram. Each and every day it pumps about 18,000 litres of blood around your body, and yet you are not normally aware that it is even beating. Run quickly upstairs, though, and you will soon feel it thumping away inside your rib cage.

A heart attack can occur when either or both sides of the heart are unable to pump sufficient blood to meet the needs of our body. Other prominent causes of a heart attack are abnormally high blood pressure (hypertension), coronary atherosclerosis (the presence of fatty deposits in the lining of the coronary arteries), and rheumatic heart disease.

A person with left-sided heart failure experiences shortness of breath after exertion, difficulty in breathing while lying down, spasms of breathlessness at night, and abnormally high pressure in the pulmonary veins. A person with right-sided failure experiences abnormally high pressure in the systemic veins, enlargement of the liver, and accumulation of fluid in the legs. A person with failure of both ventricles has an enlarged heart that beats in gallop rhythm – that is, in groups of three sounds rather than two.

FACT FILE

An electrocardiogram, or ECG, measures the electrical signals that the heart produces as it beats. These signals change when a person is suffering from certain medical conditions that affect the heart.

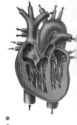

WHEN DOES THE HEART STOP BEATING?

Your heart is a muscular pump that never stops beating. It has its own timing device that produces tiny electrical signals. These signals cause the heart muscle to contract rhythmically. The pump on the right side of the heart receives blood that has been pumped around the body. This blood is dark red and has used up most of its oxygen. The right pump sends it on a short circuit through the lungs that surround the heart. The blood comes back bright red and rich in oxygen, to the heart's left side, ready for its journey around the body. When the heart stops beating, body tissues no longer receive fresh blood carrying oxygen and nutrients. So life ends.

However, in a hospital, the cardiopulmonary machine can take over the job of heart and lungs. This means doctors can resuscitate people or carry out operations on the heart, such as replacing diseased valves.

aorta

superior vena cava

pulmonary artery

pulmonary valve

pulmonary veins

atria

aortic valve

mitral valve

chordae tendineae

tricuspid valve

papillary muscle

ventricles

inferior vena cava

The heart

FACT FILE

When the body is very active, the heart can pump 20 gallons of blood each minute. That would fill a bathtub within two minutes.

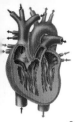

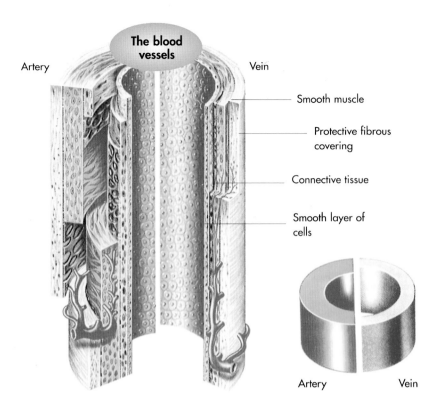

The blood vessels

Artery

Vein

Smooth muscle

Protective fibrous covering

Connective tissue

Smooth layer of cells

Artery

Vein

WHEN DOES BLOOD FLOW FROM VEINS TO ARTERIES?

Your body has an amazingly complex and delicate system of blood vessels, carrying blood to every nook and cranny, and then returning to the heart. These vessels are called arteries and veins and they are both tubes made up of four different layers. The arteries carry the blood away from the heart and the veins return it.

The veins frequently anastomose (or join together) with each other so that the blood flow can alter direction. This is caused if there is any constriction or pressure from movement of muscles or ligaments.

FACT FILE

Just over half of blood is plasma, a pale yellow, sweet-smelling, sticky fluid. It contains hundreds of dissolved substances, from sugars for energy, to hormones, to wastes like carbon dioxide.

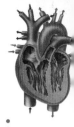

WHEN DOES THE SPLEEN PRODUCE RED BLOOD CELLS?

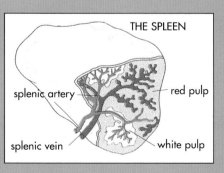

liver

spleen

lymph nodes

Blood formation

The spleen is one of the main filters of the blood. Not only do the reticular cells remove the old and worn-out blood cells, but they will also remove any abnormal cells. This applies in particular to red blood cells, but white cells and platelets are also filtered selectively by the spleen when it is necessary.

The spleen will also remove abnormal particles that are floating in the bloodstream. It therefore plays a very important part in ridding the body of harmful bacteria.

In some circumstances the spleen has a major role in the manufacture of new red blood cells. This does not happen in the normal adult, but in people who have a bone marrow disease. The spleen and liver are major sites of red blood cell production. Another function of the spleen is to manufacture a great deal of the blood of a foetus while it is in the uterus during its period of gestation.

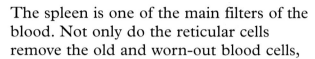

THE SPLEEN

splenic artery

red pulp

splenic vein

white pulp

FACT FILE

The spleen is situated in the top left-hand corner of the abdomen, just below the diaphragm. It is in a relatively exposed position, which is why it is frequently damaged in accidents and has to be removed.

WHEN ARE OUR BLOOD GROUPS DETERMINED?

Receptor	A	B	AB	O
Donor A				
B				
AB				
O				

Our individual blood group is determined by our parents at the time of our conception. Blood groups are determined by the presence of antigens (a substance capable of stimulating an immune response) on the surfaces of the red cells. Although the red blood cells in different people look the same they are, in fact, dissimilar. They can be divided up into four main groups: A, B, AB and O.

Blood can be transplanted from one person to another by what we call a blood transfusion. It is very important that the blood given matches the person's group, because if the wrong types of blood are mixed together the result can be serious blood clots.

FACT FILE

Blood begins to clot as soon as it is exposed to the air, plugging the wound. White blood cells gather around the wound to kill invading microbes, and new skin cells grow into the healing wound beneath the scab.

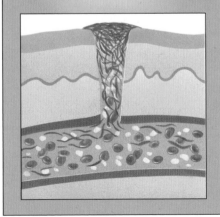

WHEN DO RED AND WHITE BLOOD CELLS DIE?

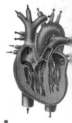

FACT FILE

An average adult body has about 5 litres of blood. At any one time, about 1,250 ml are in the arteries, 3,500 ml in the veins and about 250 ml in the capillaries. The cells in blood flow through a capillary for only half a second before they move into the next type of vessels, small veins.

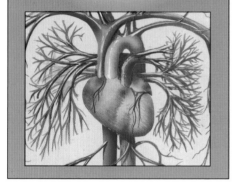

Both white and red blood cells are formed in the bone marrow. Each red blood cell measures about 7.5 microns (thousandths of a milli-metre) in diameter and is shaped a little like a doughnut. Red blood cells contain haemoglobin, which gives them their red pigment. There are 5 to 6 million red cells per cubic mm of blood. The red cell only survives about 120 days and the damaged and old cells are removed by the spleen and liver.

A white blood cell is not really white but almost transparent. It can change shape, push out folds and finger-like projections and move along by oozing and crawling like an amoeba in a pond. These cells survive less than a week.

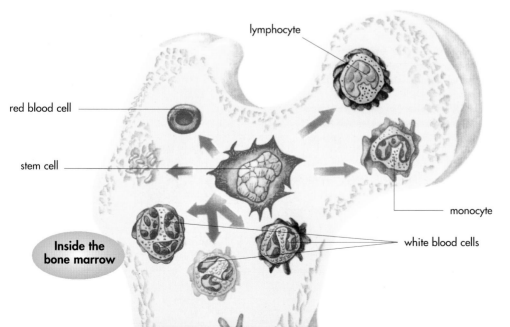

lymphocyte

red blood cell

stem cell

monocyte

white blood cells

Inside the bone marrow

WHEN DO WE LEARN TO TALK?

As air flows out of the lungs, we can use it to make the sounds of speech and other noises. At the top of the windpipe, in the sides of the voice box or larynx, are two stiff, shelf-like folds – called the vocal cords. Criss-crossed muscles in the voice box can pull them together so that air passes through a narrow slit between them and makes them vibrate, creating sounds. As the vocal cords are pulled tighter, they make higher-pitched sounds. As the vocal cords loosen, they make lower-pitched sounds. Of course, when we actually learn to talk, our speech depends on the development of the brain and its ability to copy the sounds that we hear.

FACT FILE

Although many people think of speech as our main way of communicating, we do not have to use spoken words. People who can't speak learn a language called signing, in which hands and fingers are used to signal letters and words.

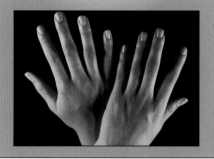

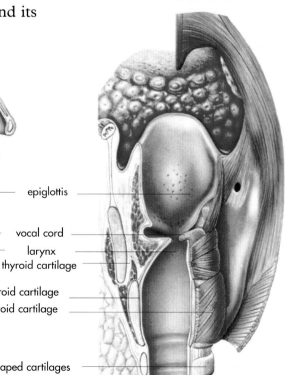

epiglottis

vocal cord

larynx
thyroid cartilage

thyroid cartilage

cricoid cartilage

Organs of speech

trachea: C-shaped cartilages

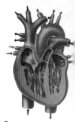

The mouth

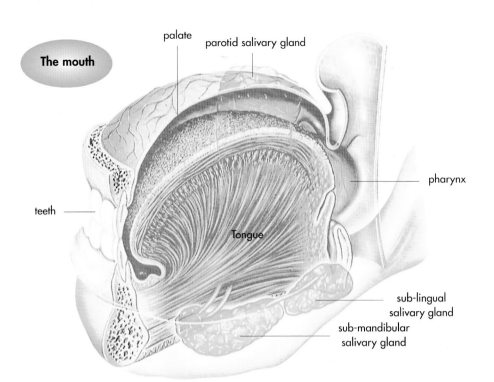

palate

parotid salivary gland

pharynx

teeth

Tongue

sub-lingual salivary gland

sub-mandibular salivary gland

WHEN DO WE PRODUCE SALIVA?

FACT FILE

The four main tastes are sweet, salt, bitter and sour, and you can taste them with different parts of your tongue. You can check where the four tastes are by dabbing it with a little salt, sugar, coffee grounds (bitter) and lemon juice (sour).

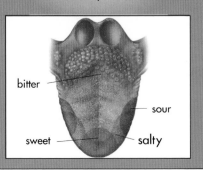

bitter

sour

sweet

salty

The major function of saliva is to help in the process of digestion. It keeps the mouth moist and comfortable when we eat and helps to moisten dry food, allowing it to be chewed and swallowed more easily. The mucus in saliva coats the bolus (or chewed food) and acts as a lubricant to help us to swallow.

The enzyme ptyalin which is found in saliva begins the first stage of digestion. It begins to break down starchy food into simpler sugars. Saliva also allows us to taste our food and drink. Each day we all usually produce about 1.7 litres (3 pints) of saliva.

55

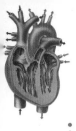

WHEN DOES FOOD REACH OUR INTESTINES?

Everything you eat has to be chopped up and broken down before the nutrients or goodness in it can be taken into your blood and used by your body cells to make energy. This takes place in your digestive system or gut. The food leaves your stomach a little at a time and goes into your small intestine. This is where most of the digestion takes place by adding digestive chemicals and absorbing the digested nutrients into the body. The lining of the intestine is folded into millions of tiny fingers called villi. Undigested food continues its journey on to the large intestine where excess water and minerals are extracted from the leftover food.

duodenum

hepatic portal vein drains digested food to the liver

branch of a mesenteric artery

muscle layers

enzyme-producing glands

FACT FILE

HOW MUCH ENERGY DO WE USE?

Sitting or lying: 43–72 cals per hour

Walking: 144–216 cals per hour

Running: 432–575 cals per hour

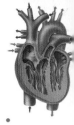

WHEN IS THE APPENDIX USED IN DIGESTION?

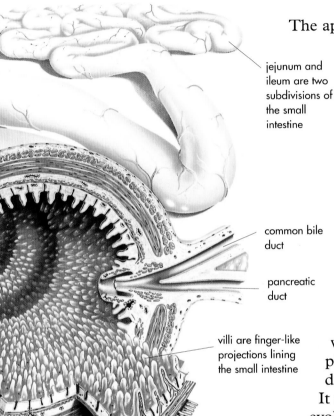

jejunum and ileum are two subdivisions of the small intestine

common bile duct

pancreatic duct

villi are finger-like projections lining the small intestine

The appendix is a narrow tube-like piece of gut resembling a tail, which is located at the end of the large intestine. The tip of the tube is closed; the other end joins on to the large intestine. It is only found in humans, certain species of apes and in the wombat.

Other animals have an organ in the same position as the appendix that acts as an additional stomach, where the fibrous part of plants and cellulose is digested by bacteria. It seems that as we evolved through the ages and began to eat less cellulose in favour of meat, a special organ was no longer needed for its digestion.

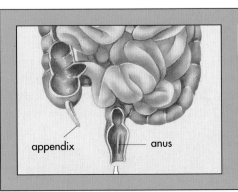

appendix   anus

FACT FILE

The only time we are aware of the appendix is when it becomes infected and this is known as appendicitis. For the most part it is a useless part of the large intestine with no known function.

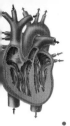

WHEN MAY THE LIVER FAIL TO FUNCTION PROPERLY?

The liver has two vital roles to play: making (or processing) new chemicals, and neutralizing poisons and waste products. The liver is the largest organ in the body weighing between 1.36 and 1.81 kg (3 and 4 lb). It is only possible for the blood to get back to the heart and lungs from the stomach by first passing through a system of veins in the liver, known as the portal system.

A variety of things including viruses, drugs, environmental pollutants, genetic disorders and systemic diseases can affect the liver and stop it functioning properly. However, the liver has a marvellous capacity to renew itself and will usually return to normal once the causes are removed or eliminated.

FACT FILE

If the kidneys do not work properly, they can become 'furred' up with hard crusts and crystals of chemicals from the urine. These deposits are called kidney stones. They can be removed by an operation, dissolved by drugs, or shattered into tiny fragments by high-energy ultrasonic sound waves.

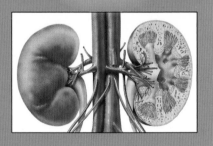

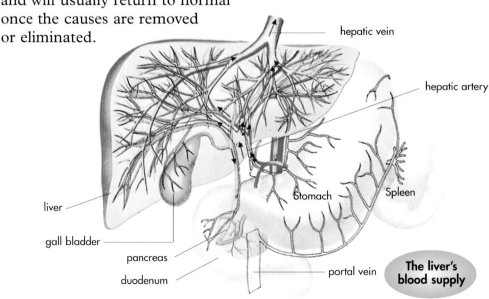

hepatic vein

hepatic artery

liver

gall bladder

pancreas

duodenum

Stomach

Spleen

portal vein

The liver's blood supply

WHEN DO WE SUFFER FROM REFERRED PAIN?

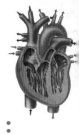

FACT FILE

Some areas of the skin are densely packed with nerve endings, as in the finger-tips, while others, as on the back, have comparatively few.

Referred pain is a pain that's source is in one place of the body but we feel it on another part of the body. Internal organs and structure are well supplied with nerves, but pain is widely spread and poorly located compared with skin sensations. Most of the pain is caused by stretching and contracting, as in the pain of colic. Internal pain will cause stimulation of local nerves in a portion of the spinal cord, and this makes it appear that the pain is coming from the skin which is supplied by the sensory nerves.

The heart (**1**) and the oesophagus (**2**) refer pain to the neck, shoulders and arms. The uterus (**3**) and pancreas (**4**) refer pain to the lumber region. The kidneys (**5**) refer pain into the groin. Pain from the diaphragm may be referred to the shoulders as the phrenic nerve is formed from the spinal nerves in the neck, which also supply the shoulders.

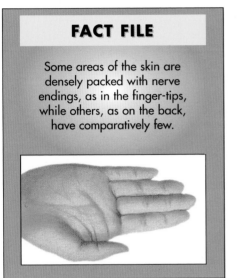

Referred pain

from the heart

from the oesophagus

pancreas and stomach

kidney

gynaeocological

1

2

4

5

3

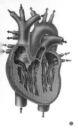

WHEN DO WE SEE IMAGES UPSIDE DOWN?

The eyes are the body's windows on the world. Like a video camera they detect a moving picture of the world and turn it into tiny electrical signals. These signals are nerve impulses which go to the brain to be sorted. In ancient times people thought that light shone out of their eyes onto what they looked at. Now we know that light rays pass from an object into the eye. Every second or two the eyelids blink and sweep tear fluid across the conjunctiva, washing away and dust and germs.

The image that forms on the retina when light passes through the lens is actually upside down. This is because of the way in which light rays are bent by the eye's lens. The brain automatically turns the image the right way up, but you are never aware that this is happening.

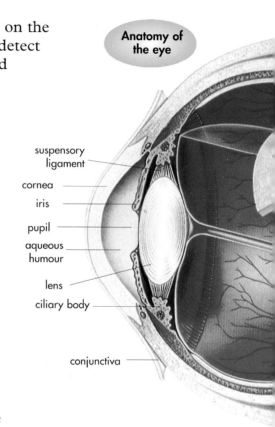

Anatomy of the eye

suspensory ligament
cornea
iris
pupil
aqueous humour
lens
ciliary body
conjunctiva

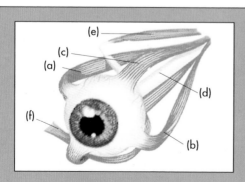

(e)
(c)
(a)
(d)
(f)
(b)

FACT FILE

There are six muscles to control the movements of each eye. Muscle (a) swivels it away from the nose; (b) towards the nose; (c) rotates it upward; (d) downwards; (e) moves it down and outwards and (f) moves it upwards and outwards.

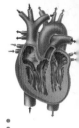

WHEN DO PEOPLE WEAR CONTACT LENSES?

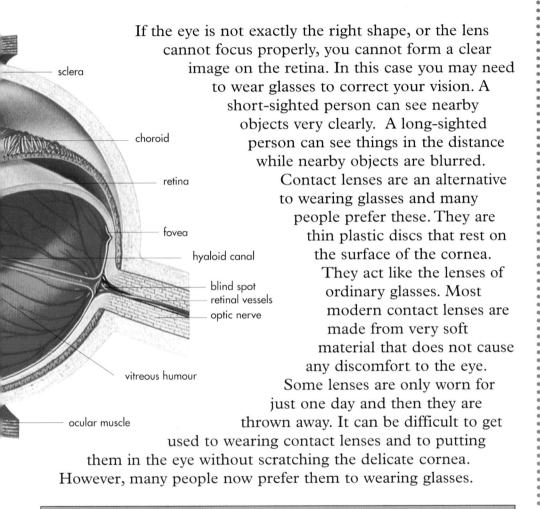

sclera

choroid

retina

fovea

hyaloid canal

blind spot
retinal vessels
optic nerve

vitreous humour

ocular muscle

If the eye is not exactly the right shape, or the lens cannot focus properly, you cannot form a clear image on the retina. In this case you may need to wear glasses to correct your vision. A short-sighted person can see nearby objects very clearly. A long-sighted person can see things in the distance while nearby objects are blurred.

Contact lenses are an alternative to wearing glasses and many people prefer these. They are thin plastic discs that rest on the surface of the cornea. They act like the lenses of ordinary glasses. Most modern contact lenses are made from very soft material that does not cause any discomfort to the eye. Some lenses are only worn for just one day and then they are thrown away. It can be difficult to get used to wearing contact lenses and to putting them in the eye without scratching the delicate cornea. However, many people now prefer them to wearing glasses.

FACT FILE

Film and television images consist of a series of rapidly changing still images, yet we see them as continuous motion. There is a slight delay between each of the images that appear on the screen. However, because this delay is so short, our brain is able to fill in the gaps and provide a complete picture of what is happening.

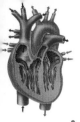

WHEN DO WE RECOGNIZE A SPECIFIC TASTE?

Tastes are detected by thousands of taste buds scattered along the tip, sides, and back of the tongue. There are also some near the lips, on the roof and sides of the mouth, and in the upper throat. Each taste bud is tiny – a microscopic bunch of about 50 cells which have furry, frilly tips. There are four main types of taste: sweet, sour, salty and bitter and these can be detected by different areas of the tongue as shown in the diagram opposite. When molecules land on the frilly tip, the tastebud cells make nerve signals. These signals pass long small nerves which gather into two main nerves – the seventh and ninth cranial nerves. These signals then travel along them to the gustatory, or taste, area in the brain. You have around 10,000 taste buds on your tongue.

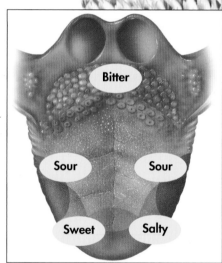

The tongue

Bitter

Sour

Sour

Sweet

Salty

olfactory bulb

skull

cilla

covering of mucus

FACT FILE

Smell enters the cavity behind the nose when you inhale. They also rise up from the back of the mouth as you eat, which is why smell is such an important part of enjoying food.

WHEN DO WE LOSE OUR SENSE OF TASTE?

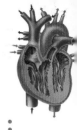

Epiglottis

Base of the tongue

Cross-section of a vallate papilla

Taste bud

Salivary glands

Cross-section of a salivary gland showing drops of saliva

FACT FILE

The human sense of smell is very poor compared to that of animals, such as dogs. Some dogs are able to identify and follow the smell of a person's perspiration.

Compared to other sensations (in particular smell) our taste sense is not very sensitive. It has been estimated that a person needs 25,000 times as much of a substance in the mouth to taste it as is needed by the smell receptors to smell it. However, despite this, the combination of the four types of taste buds responding to the basic tastes of salt, sour, bitter or sweet, enable a wide range of sensations to be determined as the brain analyzes the relative strength of the tastes. If we were to lose our sense of smell, almost all taste sensation would be lost as well. Eating oysters, for instance, where the smell is so important, would become a dull and totally 'tasteless' experience. That is why we sometimes lose our sense of taste when we have a cold because our nasal passages become blocked. You will gradually lose your sense of taste as you grow older, which is one reason why elderly people may no longer enjoy their food so much.

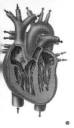

WHEN DOES OUR SENSE OF TOUCH ALERT THE BRAIN OF DANGER?

Close your eyes and touch something, such as your clothes, a table, a car or even your own skin. Stroke it gently. What does it feel like? Is it hard or soft, hot or cold? The surface may be smooth, bumpy, gritty, furry or hairy. It could be dry, moist, or slimy. Your skin continuously passes huge amounts of information to the brain. It monitors touch, pain, temperature and other factors that tell the brain exactly how the body is being affected by its environment. Without this constant flow of information, you would keep injuring yourself accidentally, which is what happens in some rare diseases where the skin senses are lost. Senses in the skin are measured by tiny receptors at the ends of nerves. There are several different types of receptor. Each type can detect only one kind of sensation, such as pain, temperature, pressure, touch and so on.

Skin sensation

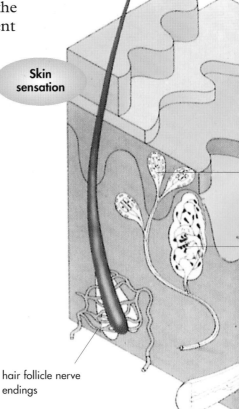

hair follicle nerve endings

FACT FILE

Sometimes we need drugs, or analgesics, to control a pain. Some drugs, such as aspirin, work by preventing the sensation of pain from reaching the brain.

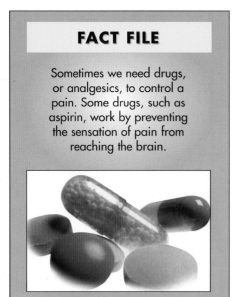

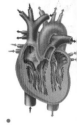

WHEN DO WE USE OUR BRAIN TO SMELL?

The part of the brain that analyzes messages coming from the receiver cells in the nose is closely connected with the limbic system, that part of the brain that deals with emotions, moods and memory. It is called the primitive brain, sometimes even the 'smelling brain'. The connection explains why smells are richly supplied with emotional significance. The smell of fresh rain on a summer's day usually makes people feel happy and invigorated, and it may also awaken happy memories. The smell of fresh-baked bread may bring on instant pangs of hunger, while the scent of perfume may remind you of a loved one. On the other hand, unpleasant smells such as rotten eggs, produce revulsion and sometimes even nausea.

Certain smells will bring memories of long forgotten special occasions flooding back. This is because we tend to remember those things which have special emotional significance. This is because the areas of the brain which process memories are also closely linked to the limbic system, which in turn is linked to the areas in the brain that control the sense of smell.

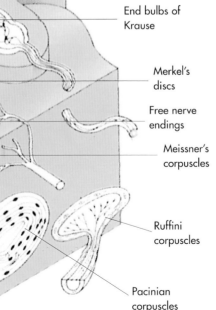

End bulbs of Krause

Merkel's discs

Free nerve endings

Meissner's corpuscles

Ruffini corpuscles

Pacinian corpuscles

FACT FILE

Aromatherapy is the art of using the perfumed essential oils of plants to treat the body and mind. The perfume passes over the nerve cells in the nasal passage and a message is sent to the brain.

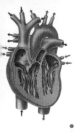

WHEN ARE BABIES DELIVERED AS A 'BREECH BIRTH'?

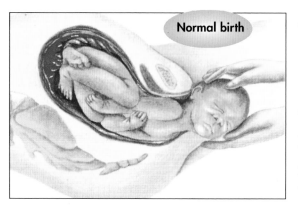

Normal birth

At about 280 days after the baby's inception, the mother starts to feel strong tightening pains, called contractions, in her womb when the birth is near. These contractions become stronger and the neck of the cervix starts to open. As the contractions continue, the baby's head moves down and eventually emerges through the cervix and vagina.

A breech birth is different to a regular birth because the buttocks engage in the pelvis instead of the head. This makes delivery more complicated as the largest part, namely the head, is delivered last. A breech birth is encountered about once in every thirty deliveries. Because the head in such cases is the last part of the child to be delivered and because this part of the delivery is the most difficult, the umbilical cord may be compressed while the after-coming head is being born, with the result that the child may be deprived of oxygen.

FACT FILE

Sometimes a baby cannot be born normally through the vagina and so it has to be surgically removed from the mother's womb. This operation is called a caesarean section.

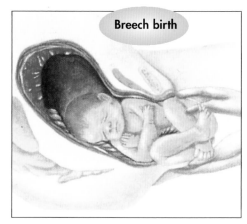

Breech birth

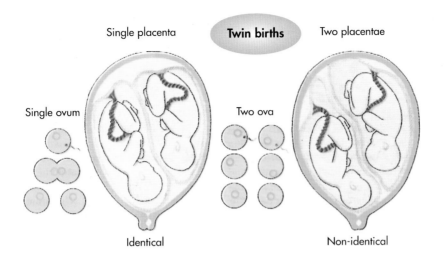

Single placenta

Twin births

Two placentae

Single ovum

Two ova

Identical

Non-identical

WHEN ARE TWINS CONCEIVED?

A baby begins as a fertilized egg – a pinhead-sized egg cell from the mother, which has joined an even smaller tadpole-shaped sperm cell from the father. Although thousands of these sperm cells may cluster around the egg cell, only one of these will actually fertilize the egg.

Non-identical twins are produced when two eggs are released at the same time, and both are fertilized. They can be the same sex, or brother and sister.

Identical twins are produced when the embryo splits into two in the early stages of its development. This produces two identical children of the same sex. Some identical twins look so alike that they can only be told apart by their fingerprints.

Only one in 83 pregnancies results in twins.

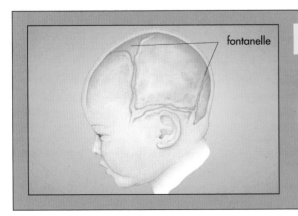

fontanelle

FACT FILE

The bones of a baby's head are not fully fused at birth, allowing the skull to pass through the mother's birth canal. The bones gradually become joined, but a gap at the top of the skull, called the fontanelle, may not close up for several months.

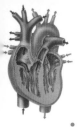

WHEN DOES RESPIRATION OCCUR?

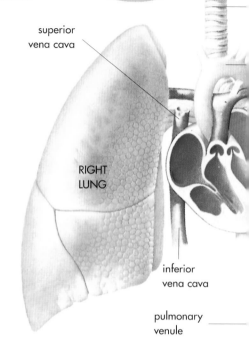

The lungs

superior
vena cava

RIGHT
LUNG

inferior
vena cava

pulmonary
venule

FACT FILE

The average person at rest breathes in and out about 10–14 times per minute. If you sing or play instruments like trumpets, you need lots of puff. Learn to use the muscle under your lungs to get more lung power.

Respiration, or breathing, is when you draw air in through the nose and mouth and into the lungs. Like all movements in the body, those of respiration rely on muscle power. There are two main sets of breathing muscles: the intercostal muscle and the diaphragm. Breathe in deeply and watch your ribs rise and your chest expand. Together these muscles make the chest bigger and stretch the spongy lungs inside. As the lungs enlarge, they suck in air down the windpipe. This is how we breathe in. Then the muscles relax. The ribs fall back down and the diaphragm resumes its domed shape as the spongy, elastic lungs spring back to their smaller size. The lungs blow some of their air up the windpipe. This is how we breathe out.

    The movements of breathing are controlled by the brain. It sends out signals to make the muscles contract. The signals pass along nerves to the intercostal and diaphragm muscles, making them contract. This happens every few seconds throughout our life, even when you are asleep.

WHEN DO WE COUGH?

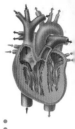

larynx

trachea

aorta

pulmonary artery

left main bronchus

small bronchus

terminal bronchiole

Coughing is the way in which the lungs dislodge anything that blocks the air passages. Usually these are only minor blockages caused by a build-up of mucus when you have a cold or chest infection. When you cough, your vocal cords press together to seal off the air passages. At the same time your chest muscles become tense, raising the pressure in your lungs. When you release the air it rushes out, carrying the obstruction with it.

The delicate alveoli inside the lungs can be damaged by many different things, thus causing us to cough. One is tobacco smoke, which clogs the alveoli and airways with thick tar. Others are the polluting gases that hover in the air of many big cities, coming from vehicle exhausts as well as factory and power-plant chimneys. Some types of industrial dust and particles floating in the air, such as asbestos or coal-mine dust can cause considerable damage to the lungs.

FACT FILE

It can be quite hard to breathe when you are at the top of a mountain. At high altitudes the air is thinner so there is not so much oxygen in it. This means that you will breathe heavily if you exert yourself by climbing.

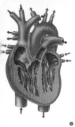

WHEN DO WE LOSE OUR MILK TEETH?

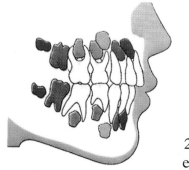

Milk teeth

The average person has two sets of teeth, one after the other. The first is the baby, milk, or deciduous set. Even before birth, teeth appear as tiny buds below the gums. They begin to erupt, or show above the gum from the age of a few months. By the age of about three all 20 first teeth have usually appeared. In each half (left and right) of each jaw (upper and lower), there are two incisors, one canine, and two molars.

From about the age of six years, the first teeth start to fall out. These are replaced by the adult, second, or permanent set. First are usually the front incisors and the first molars, at around seven to eight years. Last are the rear-most molars, or wisdom teeth. They appear at 18–20 years of age in some people, while in others they erupt at 40 or 50 years of age – and sometimes they never appear. In each half of each jaw, there are typically two incisors, one canine, two premolars, and three molars, making a full set of 32 teeth.

FACT FILE

Your back teeth are bumpy on top. You can feel it. They work together, grinding food between the bumps. These grinders need regular and careful cleaning when they finish work. Food often sticks between the bumps.

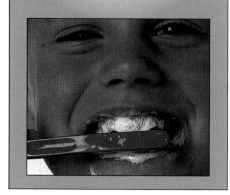

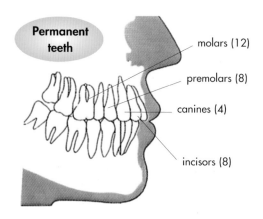

Permanent teeth

molars (12)

premolars (8)

canines (4)

incisors (8)

When do we need fillings?

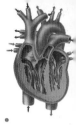

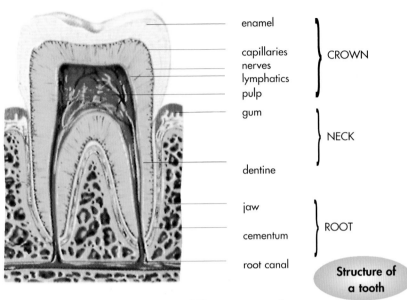

enamel

capillaries } CROWN
nerves
lymphatics
pulp

gum

} NECK

dentine

jaw

} ROOT
cementum

root canal

Structure of a tooth

Each tooth has two main parts. The root anchors it firmly in the gum, to withstand the tremendous pressures that are exerted when you bite and chew hard foods like nuts. The crown is the visible part above the gum. It is covered with whitish enamel, which is the hardest substance in the entire body. Under the enamel is a layer of dentine, which is not quite so hard, and absorbs shocks and knocks. In the middle of the tooth are blood vessels, providing nourishment to the tooth's parts and layers, and nerves, to detect pressure and pain.

Regular visits to the dentist are important for healthy teeth. If you don't look after your teeth, they may go bad and decay. That means that they may have to be filled or even taken out by the dentist.

FACT FILE

Germs live in the holes of bad teeth. They eat the good part, which makes the holes deeper. Dentists have to drill out this germy part. The hard outside of teeth cannot grow back. Dentists have to fill the holes with metal to keep the germs out.

OUR

WORLD

CONTENTS

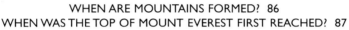

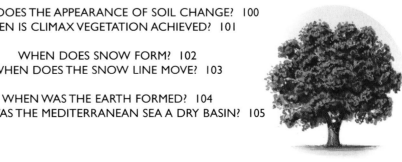

WHEN IS SUMMER SOLSTICE?

The earth revolves around the Sun and at the same time it revolves on its own axis. As it moves around the Sun, it is also spinning like a top. If the axis of the earth were at right angles to the path of the Earth around the sun, all the days of the year would be the same length. However, the earth is tilted at an angle of 66.5°. In June the northern hemisphere is tilted towards the Sun and it receives more sunshine during a day. This is its warmest season called summer. On the 21 June the Sun is directly over the Tropic of Cancer and it is midsummer in the Northern hemisphere. This is the time known as the summer solstice.

FACT FILE

The Sun is the source of light and heat for the solar system. The four planets closest to the Sun are small and solid, the closest being Mercury. An asteroid belt separates these from the four larger planets which are made up of gas.

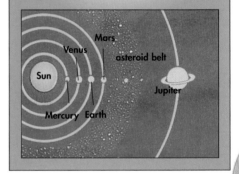

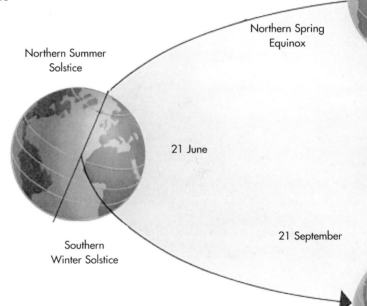

Northern Summer Solstice

Northern Spring Equinox

21 June

21 September

Southern Winter Solstice

Southern Spring Equinox

WHEN IS THE SHORTEST DAY?

FACT FILE

Mars is known as the 'Red Planet' because it is covered by a stone desert that contains lots of iron oxide, making it appear rusty red. The water and oxygen that used to exist on Mars are now locked up in these iron deposits; nowadays the planet has hardly any atmosphere.

The shortest day of the year is in the winter solstice which is 21 December. When the Northern Hemisphere is turned toward the Sun, the countries north of the equator have their summer season, and the countries south of the equator have their winter season. When the direct rays of the Sun fall on the southern hemisphere, it is their summer and it is winter in the northern hemisphere. There are two days in the year when night and day are equal all over the world. They come in the spring and fall, just halfway between the two solstices. One is the autumnal equinox in September, and the other is the spring equinox in March.

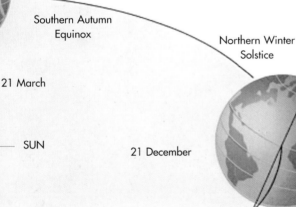

Southern Autumn Equinox

Northern Winter Solstice

21 March

SUN

21 December

Southern Summer Solstice

Northern Spring Equinox

WHEN DOES A LUNAR ECLIPSE OCCUR?

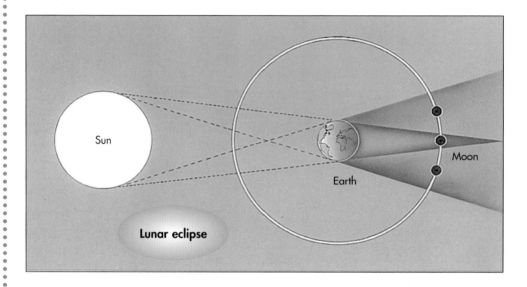

Sun

Earth

Moon

Lunar eclipse

The Earth casts a long shadow into space, and when this shadow passes over the Moon it can cause an eclipse.

A lunar eclipse can only happen during a full Moon, when the Sun is directly behind the Earth. It happens only occasionally, because the orbit of the Moon is slightly tilted and so the shadow usually misses it. Lunar eclipses can last for over one hour, but they do not completely black out the shadowed part of the Moon. Some sunlight always filters through, making the shadow look a reddish-brown colour. Eclipses can only be seen from certain parts of the world.

FACT FILE

The distance of the Moon away from the Earth was settled once and for all after the Apollo astronauts left a small reflector on the Moon's surface. This distance is 384,000 km, though it varies slightly because the Moon does not have a perfectly circular orbit.

WHEN DOES A SOLAR ECLIPSE OCCUR?

The Moon is 400 times smaller than the Sun but about 400 times closer. So we see them both as about the same size.

A solar eclipse is when the Moon blocks out the light from the Sun. This can make the day turn dark as all the light from the Sun is blocked out in a total eclipse. In a partial eclipse only part of the light is blocked out.

The Sun is our nearest star. It is 149.6 million km (92.9 million miles) away from Earth. It is the heat and light from the Sun that makes life on Earth possible. The huge gravity pull of the Sun keeps the planets of our solar system orbiting around it.

TELL ME WHEN : OUR WORLD

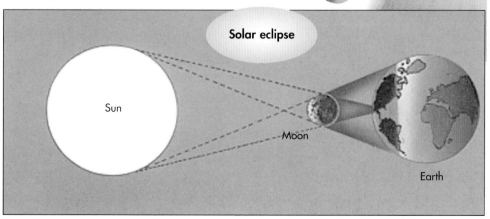

Solar eclipse

Sun

Moon

Earth

WHEN DO THE OCEANS FREEZE?

In Antarctica and the Arctic, the oceans freeze because the temperatures are so low. Seawater, unlike fresh water, continues to increase in density as its temperature decreases towards freezing point (about −1.8°C). In fact Antarctica contains 90 per cent of all the ice on the Earth. Scientists have calculated that should all this ice melt, sea levels would rise by 60m causing world-wide flooding. An accumulation of sea ice can cause an iceberg which floats in the sea because it is less dense than water.

FACT FILE

Over 360 million square kilometres of the Earth's surface area are covered by oceans and seas, with the Pacific accounting for nearly 36% of the total.

An iceberg in a frozen ocean

WHEN DO WAVES BREAK?

Some sort of force or energy is needed to start a wave, and it is the wind that provides this energy in the water. Wind blows the surface layers of the sea, gradually forming a rolling movement of waves. As these waves near the coast, the sea-bed interrupts their rolling movement and they mount up and break onto the beach. The water inside a wave moves round and round in a circle. Near the shore, the circular shape of the wave is changed and it becomes squashed. The top of the wave becomes unstable, so when it hits the beach, it topples and spills over. On beaches with a shallow slope the waves pile up to a great height before breaking, causing surf.

FACT FILE

For centuries sailors have been in terror of being sucked into a whirlpool that would swallow them and their ships. Whirlpools happen when opposing currents meet.

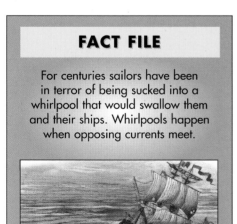

WHEN CAN WATER WEAR AWAY SOLID ROCK?

FACT FILE

When water seeps through the ground and reaches hot rock or volcanic gases, it boils violently. This produces steam that can shoot the water out of cracks, causing a geyser.

Water itself cannot wear away rock, but tiny particles of grit carried in the water can eventually wear away the hardest of rocks. It is this continuous wearing process that cuts valleys through mountains and hills. The faster the water flows, the more grit it carries, and consequently wears away at the rock to a greater extent. The same process can be seen along the coast. These rocks are worn away by the constant action of sand dashed against them by the waves.

WHEN DO RIVERS RUN BACKWARDS?

Reversed flowing water

In the former Soviet Union the direction of several rivers was diverted or even reversed to provide water for irrigation. Some of the rivers running into the Aral Sea were diverted northwards in a huge water management project to irrigate land north of the region. In some cases the direction of their flow was reversed. The result was that the Aral Sea began to dry up because no more river water flowed into it.

Sometimes the flow is reversed naturally, but this only happens in very large rivers, when very high tides overcome the normal river currents. In narrow parts of the river valley the water begins to pile up, and eventually a wave called a tidal bore passes back up the river, sometimes for a great distance.

FACT FILE

Tidal bores happen in the Amazon in South America, where there is a bore as high as 4.5 metres. A smaller bore travels up the River Severn in England.

WHEN DO EARTHQUAKES OCCUR?

Our planet is a very restless place. Every 30 seconds, the ground suddenly rumbles and trembles. Most of the movements are so slight that they are not felt. Others can be so large they cause complete disaster. Big cracks appear in the land, streets buckle and buildings simply crumble. In fact whole towns and cities can be destroyed. These are called earthquakes and the reason they occur is because the Earth's crust is made up of moving parts called plates. When these plates slide past or into each other, the rocks jolt and send out shock waves.

FACT FILE

Both mining and tunnelling operations are known to have caused earthquakes in areas that are already under tension due to movements in the Earth's crust.

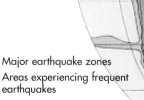

Major earthquake zones

Areas experiencing frequent earthquakes

WHEN DO WE USE A SEISMOGRAPH?

FACT FILE

The edges of the Pacific plate are surrounded by earthquakes, volcanic activity and hot springs, caused by the crust shifts and hot lava rises near the surface.

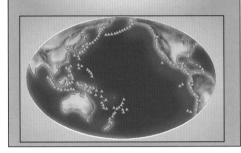

Sometimes there is a big news story about an earthquake that happened in some distant part of the world. Although people living in that area didn't feel the earth shake, scientists probably made a complete and exact record of that earthquake. They have special instruments called seismographs. The study of earthquakes is called seismology. The seismograph picks up the vibrations which are caused by one rock mass rubbing against the other. The energy of this rubbing is changed to vibration in the rocks. This vibration can travel many thousands of miles.

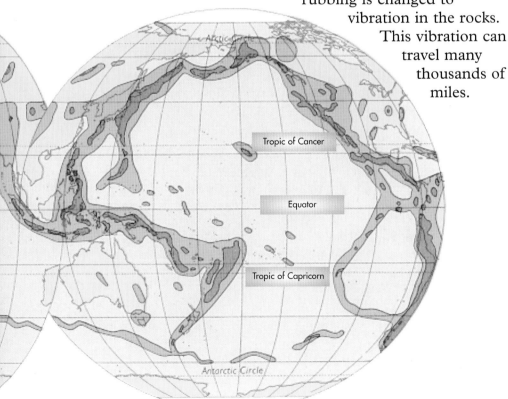

Tropic of Cancer

Equator

Tropic of Capricorn

Arctic Circle

Antarctic Circle

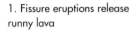

Different types of volcanic eruption

1. Fissure eruptions release runny lava

2. In Hawaiian eruptions the lava is less fluid and produces low cones

3. Vulcanian eruptions are more violent and eject solid lava

WHEN ARE VOLCANOES DORMANT?

The word *dormant* actually means 'sleeping'. So when people talk about a volcano being dormant, it really means it is temporarily sleeping and might erupt at any time in the future. An *extinct* volcano, on the other hand, is one that will not become active again. Like earthquakes, volcanoes mainly occur along fault lines. Molten rock, gases and ash are forced out through a gap in the Earth's crust to release the pressure that has built up. When there is very little pressure the volcano can remain in a dormant state for many, many years. On the island of Maui there is a volcano called Haleakala which rises to a height of about 10,025 feet. It is the world's largest inactive volcano. Its crater is about 20 miles around and some 2,720 feet deep.

FACT FILE

A major volcanic eruption can hurl boulders high into the air. These boulders, called volcanic bombs, can be very large indeed.

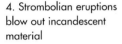

4. Strombolian eruptions blow out incandescent material

5. In the Peléean type a blocked vent is cleared explosively

6. A Plinian eruption is a continuous blast of gas that rises to immense heights

WHEN WAS THE WORST VOLCANIC ERUPTION?

The island of Krakatau, Indonesia (west of Java) was a small volcanic island. The volcano itself had laid dormant for over 200 years until August 1883. On May 20 one of the cones erupted violently and three months later the whole island blew up. It was the biggest explosion in recorded history. For two and a half days the island was in total darkness because of the amount of dust in the air. A cloud of ash rose 80 km into the air. The eruption caused a tidal wave which killed 36,000 people. The explosion could be heard and felt in Australia, 3,500 km away.

FACT FILE

On August 24 in the year AD 79, there was a great eruption of Mount Vesuvius, a volcano in southern Italy. The lava, stones, and ashes thrown up by the volcano completely buried two nearby towns.

WHEN ARE MOUNTAINS FORMED?

Mountains can be formed in three different ways. Volcanoes form mountains when lava from deep inside the Earth cools and hardens on the surface.

Other mountains are formed when two plates move towards each other under pressure or where an oceanic plate is pushed under a continental crust. The pressure causes the ground near the joining plate margins to fault and fold. The ground is forced upwards to form mountains. The Rockies, Alps, Andes, Urals and Himalayas were all formed in this way.

Finally the Earth's crust can fracture and create faults which means that large blocks of land can be moved upwards or downwards. Faults in the rocks normally occur when there is a lot of pressure on the rocks. Mountain building is a slow process and happens over centuries.

FACT FILE

Rockslides are common where forests have been destroyed on mountainsides. There are no longer any tree roots to stabilize the loose material.

Three ways in which a mountain can form

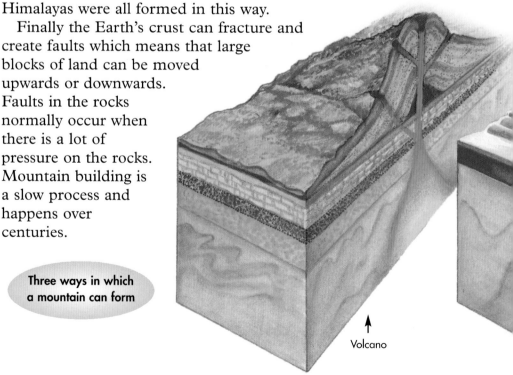

Volcano

WHEN WAS THE TOP OF MOUNT EVEREST FIRST REACHED?

FACT FILE

Mountain peaks are often seen to be surrounded by layers of cloud. This is because as winds laden with water are blown towards the mountains, they are forced to rise and the temperature drops. The water condenses into clouds at these higher altitudes.

Mount Everest, which is in the Himalayas, is 8,863 metres high. At these altitudes, mountains are always covered in snow and ice, and there is little oxygen to breathe. Mount Everest was finally conquered on May 29, 1953, when a Nepalese guide, Tenzing Norgay, and a New Zealander, Edmund Hillary, reached the highest point on the Earth's surface. Since then, many people have climbed Everest, and all the world's major peaks have now been conquered.

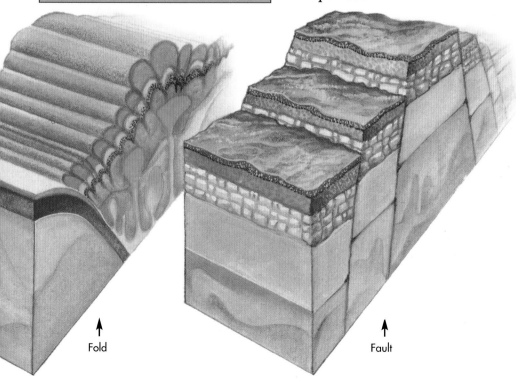

Fold

Fault

WHEN DO MONSOONS OCCUR?

A monsoon is a season of very heavy rain falling in tropical countries. Monsoons are most common near the Equator. They occur when seasonal winds spring up carrying moist air in from the sea. Important crops such as rice depend entirely on the monsoon season to provide the right growing conditions.

   If the monsoon rains fail, famine often follows. There are also some special winds called monsoon winds. These are winds that change their direction with the season. In India, the monsoons blow south as hot, dry winds in the wintertime, and blow north in the summer, bringing heavy rainfall.

Mist over high ground

FACT FILE

The Aborigines believe that if a possum is left cooking by the water's edge, a sizzling sound is produced. This noise irritates the rainbow snake, who they believe crawls underground towards the source of the noise. As it moves along, the weather turns stormy, and the monsoon rains begin.

WHEN DO FOG AND MIST ARISE?

It is tiny water droplets condensing from moist air that cause fog and mist to rise. The water droplets can occur at ground level. The air can only hold a limited amount of water. If the air suddenly cools, its capacity to hold water is reduced, which results in a mist or fog.

When fog develops, visibility can be affected quite badly. Mist is less dense. It often occurs on calm, clear nights when heat rises, forming a thin layer of mist close to the ground. Mist often forms over water because a mass of warm air passes over a cold stretch of water.

Sometimes visibility is affected in built up areas due to mist and fog, but this is sometimes mistaken for smog. Smog is a build up of exhaust fumes and factory smoke which hangs over the area until a huge amount of air movement can blow the smog away.

WHEN IS A BAROMETER USED?

A barometer is used to measure the changes in air pressure. Air pressure varies across different parts of the Earth's surface, and these differences cause winds. Air moves from an area of high pressure, or an anticyclone, to an area of low pressure, or a depression. Depressions are usually associated with worsening weather conditions and rain. In a mercury barometer the air pressure pushes down on the mercury, which is forced up the barometer to give an accurate reading.

Air pressure is greatest at sea level, where it amounts to 14.7 pounds a square inch. It is greatest there because that is the bottom of the atmosphere. At higher altitudes the pressure is less.

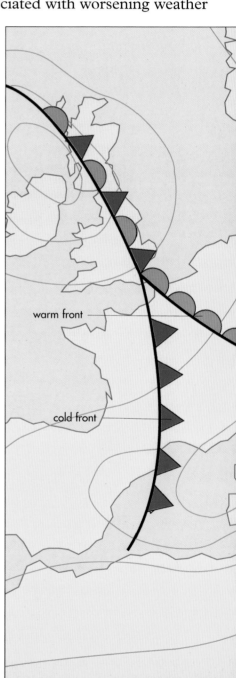

warm front

cold front

FACT FILE

The higher we go the less air pressure there is. This is the reason that space suits and the cabins of high-flying planes are pressurized. They are designed to maintain the air pressure our bodies must have.

WHEN DID WEATHER FORECASTING BEGIN?

People have been able to forecast the weather for hundreds of years. Meteorologists have used simple instruments like thermometers, rain gauges, barometers and wind gauges for many years, but with the arrival of satellite photography, weather forecasting has been transformed. With the use of computers, increasingly accurate forecasting is now possible.

Traditional forecasters have been known to use pine cones, which open and close according to the humidity of the air. An open cone is supposed to mean dry weather. Seaweed also responds to changes in humidity. Dry seaweed indicates dry weather.

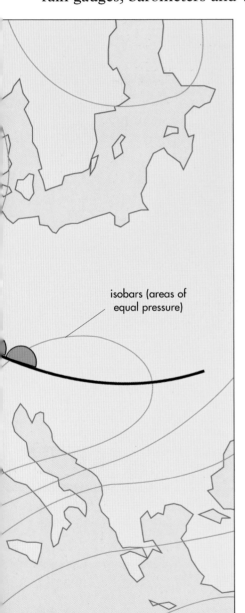

isobars (areas of equal pressure)

FACT FILE

There is an old saying regarding the weather:

If the oak tree has its leaves before the ash then it will be a fine summer.

WHEN DO WE SEE MIRAGES?

Mirages form in hot deserts where the air is so hot it bends and distorts light rays. The shimmering images that a mirage produces have often tricked travellers in deserts. People think that they can see an oasis or town on the horizon, but in reality it is not there.

Under certain conditions, such as a stretch of pavement or desert air heated by intense sunshine, the air rapidly cools with elevation and therefore increases in density and refractive power. Sunlight reflected downward from the top of an object, for example the camel above, will be directed through the cool air in the normal way. When the sky is the object of the mirage, the land is mistaken for a lake or sheet of water.

FACT FILE

About one-third of the world's land surface is covered by desert. Deserts are found wherever there is too little water to allow much plant life to grow. Salt deserts form when shallow seas and lakes dry up, leaving a deposit of smooth salt.

WHEN ARE DESERTS COLD?

About one-third of the world's land surface is covered by desert. Not all these deserts are hot and arid.

Antarctica is the biggest cold desert in the world. The blanket of two-km-thick ice covering the Tundra, howling winds and freezing temperatures stop plants and land-living animals from surviving. But the ocean around this frozen desert is full of fish and krill, so the coasts are home to millions of birds. Once the Antarctic winter sun sets, it is dark for more than two months.

The Gobi desert in Mongolia and western China is also very cold in the winter, when temperatures drop below freezing. However, the temperature in the summer is hot.

FACT FILE

One of the animals that has survived the Arctic conditions is the polar bear. In very cold climates, animals need excellent insulation to stop their body heat from escaping. This can be in the form of dense hair, fur or feathers, or on the inside, in the form of a thick layer of fat or blubber.

The Tundra

WHEN DOES THE SUN STOP SHINING?

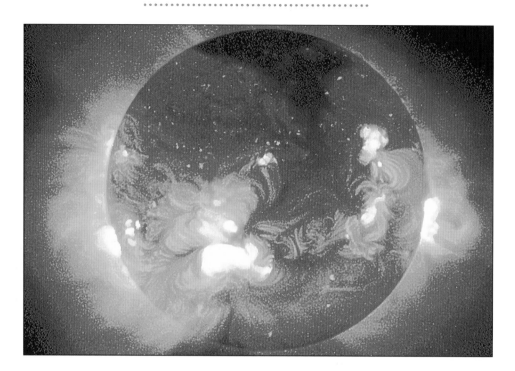

The Sun is our nearest star. Stars are massive nuclear reactors generating energy in their cores. It is the heat and light from the Sun that makes life on Earth possible. The Sun for us is a pretty steady and dependable thing. Whether we can see it or not, we know it is always there, and the answer to this question is – the Sun NEVER stops shining.

As the Earth spins on its axis, the Sun always shines on one side giving us daylight. Another time when the Sun is not visible is during a solar eclipse. This is when the Moon blocks the Sun's light from the Earth, so that the Sun seems to disappear.

FACT FILE

The direction of the Earth's rotation means that the Sun appears to rise in the east and set in the west. The Earth rotates towards the east, so the Sun first becomes visible from that direction.

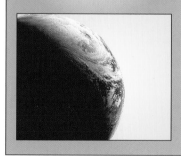

WHEN WAS THE LONGEST HEATWAVE?

The longest heatwave ever recorded was in Marble Bar, Australia when the temperature stayed above 38°C. It lasted for 162 days from 23 October 1923 to 7 April 1924.

The highest average annual temperature recorded is 34.4°C in Dallol, Ethiopia.

The lowest recorded temperature (outside of the poles) was –68°C in Verkhoyansk, Siberia, on 6 February 1933.

The lowest average annual temperature of –56.6°C was recorded at the Plateau Station, Antarctica.

FACT FILE

Some living things have adapted to survive long periods of time without water. Plants such as cacti have the ability to conserve water. They also minimize water loss as they have no leaves, and photosynthesis takes place in the stem. They have roots which reach deep into the ground for water.

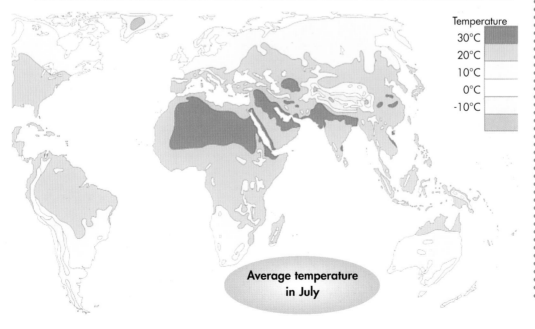

Temperature
30°C
20°C
10°C
0°C
-10°C

Average temperature
in July

WHEN DOES WATER BECOME SALTY?

TELL ME WHEN : OUR WORLD

FACT FILE

Lighthouses were built to warn ships at sea that they were approaching land and rocky water. Their beam of light across the waves made travelling by boat much safer.

Water becomes salty when minerals (including salts) dissolve into it. This process begins when rainwater falls on the land and erodes rock. The minerals found in rock are dissolved into the rainwater.

These dissolved minerals in the rainwater enter streams and rivers, gradually working their way into the seas and oceans.

This is a process which is constantly taking place, so the level and concentration of salt in the oceans and seas is always increasing. Some of the minerals are consumed by organisms in the water, but the vast majority of them make up the saltiness of the water.

WHEN WAS THE LONGEST DROUGHT?

The longest drought in recorded history took place in Calama, in the Atacama desert of Northern Chile. For four centuries, beginning in 1571, no rain fell in the area. It was not until 1971 that rainfall was first recorded again. The Atacama desert, which lies between the Andes and the Pacific ocean, is recognized as the driest place in the world.

The Atacama desert remains so dry because it lies in a region where there is constant high air pressure, with little air movement, and with few clouds overhead

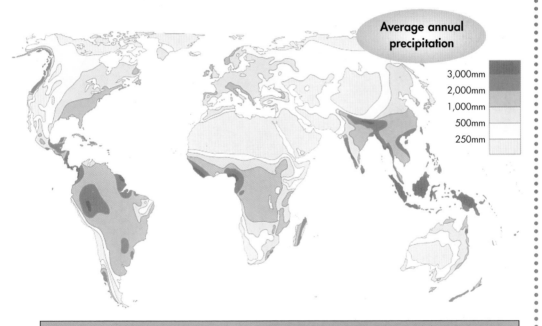

Average annual precipitation

3,000mm
2,000mm
1,000mm
500mm
250mm

FACT FILE

Some people believe that animals are good predictors of weather. One such belief is that if cows are standing in their field, then dry weather is expected. If they are lying down, however, rain is expected.

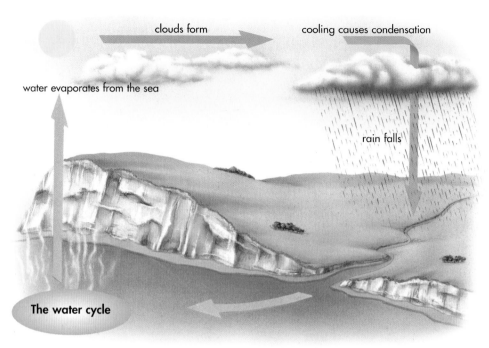

clouds form

cooling causes condensation

water evaporates from the sea

rain falls

The water cycle

WHEN DOES THE WATER CYCLE STOP?

Water cycles demonstrate how water evaporates from the oceans then rises in the air to form clouds. In areas of low pressure, the clouds release the water as rain. This falls into the oceans again, or falls onto the land where it gradually works its way back into the oceans via streams and rivers. This is a continual, cyclical process.

However, in some areas of the world where there is no rainfall for long periods of time, local water cycles *do* stop. When one event in the cycle fails to happen, the cycle breaks down.

But water can neither be created nor destroyed – it will always exist in some form. If you consider the world as a whole, with one big water cycle, the processes involved are always occurring somewhere: this cycle never stops.

FACT FILE

Too much rainwater can have disastrous effects on the land. Flooding washes away fertile soil, and begins eroding the land.

WHEN DO RIVERS BEGIN?

There are two main ways in which rivers begin. Some rivers start when a natural spring releases water from underground. These are often small trickles of water which develop into small streams. In turn these streams increase in size until they are acknowledged as rivers.

Other rivers begin when persistent rain makes a groove or a channel in a piece of land. As more and more rain falls into this channel, a flow of water slowly begins. Just like the springs, a stream can soon develop into a river.

spring

FACT FILE

When rivers reach land close to sea level, they begin to meander, forming a snake-like shape on the land. This is caused by the gradual dropping of the sediment it carries where the flow is weak.

WHEN DOES THE APPEARANCE OF SOIL CHANGE?

Soil changes its appearance when the biological or chemical make-up of it varies. For example, red soil is found in areas where there is a high content of iron compounds. Oxisol is a good example of this; it is found in tropical regions where both chemical and biological activity are high. It is illustrated in picture 5 below.

The illustrations below shows different types of soils. You can see that the appearance changes enormously. Picture 1 is tundra soil which is very dark and peaty. Picture 2 is soil belonging to desert regions; these areas tend to be unsuitable for plant growth, so this soil is lacking in nutrients and organic matter. The light-brown soils 3 and 4 are common in grassland areas. In contrast, soils 6,7,8 and 9 are typical of Northern climates where there is heavy rainfall and slow evaporation. These richer soils are suitable for abundant plant growth.

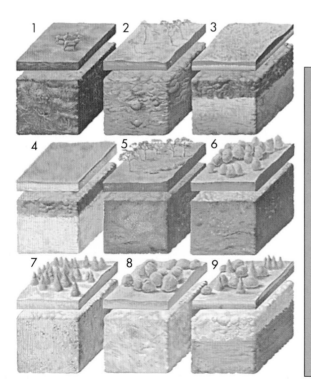

Different types of soil

FACT FILE

Soil is not just a single, consistent layer of material. Below the surface, there are different parts to soil

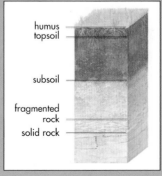

humus
topsoil

subsoil

fragmented
rock
solid rock

WHEN IS CLIMAX VEGETATION ACHIEVED?

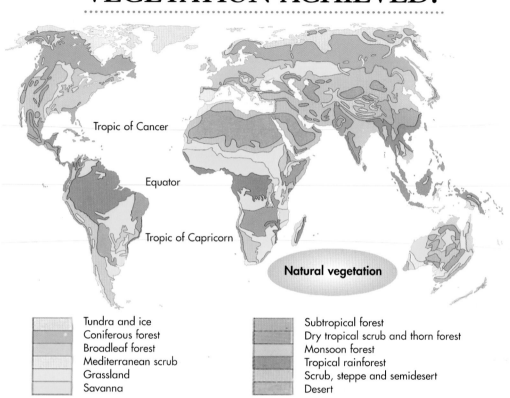

Tropic of Cancer

Equator

Tropic of Capricorn

Natural vegetation

Tundra and ice
Coniferous forest
Broadleaf forest
Mediterranean scrub
Grassland
Savanna

Subtropical forest
Dry tropical scrub and thorn forest
Monsoon forest
Tropical rainforest
Scrub, steppe and semidesert
Desert

When vegetation first starts growing in newly formed soil, it is at a disadvantage because the soil will not be nutrient-rich. As the plants die, they enrich the soil, allowing more plants to take advantage of this. As the soil gets older, it has gleaned more and more nutrients from dead plants – and more and more plants are able to grow successfully in the soil. Climax vegetation occurs when the vegetation is totally suited to the soil in the given climate. In reality, this can never last permanently due to the ever-changing environment.

FACT FILE

Rainforests have developed in areas where the soil is very fertile and where there is a great deal of rainfall. The varied vegetation suggests the soil is extremely nutrient-rich.

WHEN DOES WATER TURN INTO SNOW?

Water turns into snow at temperatures above -40°C. Snow forms when water in clouds freezes into tiny ice crystals. This moist air freezes around minute dust particles or chemical substances floating in the clouds. These particles become the core, or the nucleus, of each crystal. Snow crystals grow in size when more water crystallizes around a particular nucleus. This happens more if the air is humid.

Snow flakes are formed when a number of crystals join together in clusters. The structure of snowflakes is often a beautiful, hexagonal form. It is believed that no two snowflakes can be identical. These fall from the clouds onto land as snow.

FACT FILE

Eskimos live in houses made completely of snow called igloos. The Eskimos cut away blocks of snow and build the igloo as though they are bricks. Because where they are built is so cold, the igloos do not melt.

WHEN DOES THE SNOW LINE MOVE?

FACT FILE

Mountains such as these, the Rockies in South America, do not see a dramatic movement in the snow line. This is because they are so high up. The climate is very cold in winter and the summers are short-lived.

Snow lines are clearly visible on mountains. They mark out the area above which a mountain is permanently covered in snow.

The highest points of a mountain are much colder than the lower points. The snow which falls on the higher regions never thaws because it is so cold. In the summer, however, the warmer weather begins to melt some of the snow. This causes the snow line to move up the mountain.

As the summer months pass by and the winter months return, the snow line moves further down the mountain once again.

In colder regions, the snow line is close to ground level, but where the air is warmer, the snow line is closer to the Equator.

WHEN WAS THE EARTH FORMED?

No one knows for certain when the Earth was formed exactly. However, scientists have reasoned that it probably formed about 6,000 million years ago. This figure is twice as long as when the first signs of life are believed to have appeared on Earth, about 3,000 million years ago.

The most scientific reasoning for the creation of Earth is that it began as a huge ball of hot gases which cooled to form the planet. Seas of dissolved chemicals would have covered the land, and the air would have been an atmosphere of different gases. The atmosphere was thought to have consisted of swirling gaseous clouds which most likely caused huge electrical storms.

The poisonous gases in the atmosphere must have reacted to produce oxygen, which triggered off the first beginnings of life on Earth.

FACT FILE

As Earth cooled down, it gave off clouds of steam and gas. The moisture in these clouds eventually turned to rain, which formed the first seas.

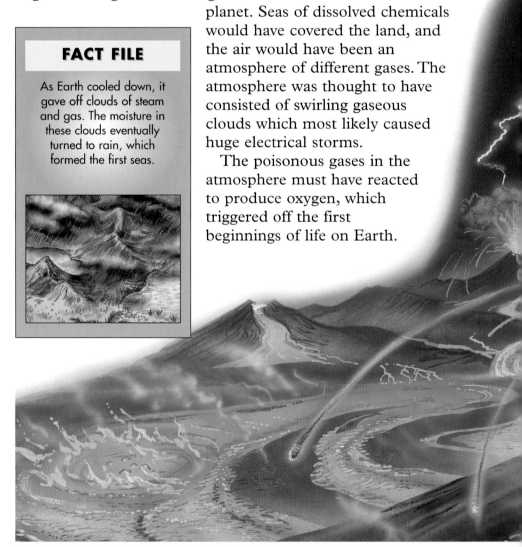

WHEN WAS THE MEDITERRANEAN A DRY BASIN?

We know the Mediterranean today as a huge sea off the coast of Europe. However, the Mediterranean was not always like that. Approximately 5 million years ago, the Mediterranean was a dry basin. Movements in the Earth's crust opened up the Gibraltar Straits between the continental areas which are now Africa and Europe. The Atlantic Ocean would have poured through this new opening into the dry basin. The result would have been an enormous waterfall, nearly 800 metres high. So much water poured in from the Atlantic that the Mediterranean Sea was created in only a few years.

FACT FILE

Of course, through time the shape of the continents will continue to change, and new seas will form; some could even join together. Below shows what the Earth may look like in the future.

150 million years' time

Present day

THE NATURAL

WORLD

CONTENTS

• •

WHEN DID DARWIN SAIL TO THE GALAPAGOS ISLANDS?

The marine iguana

In the year 1831 Charles Darwin (1809–1882) set out on an exploratory voyage in the ship *Beagle*, heading for South America. The voyage lasted five years and during this time Darwin kept careful notes of everything he saw, in particular the strange animal life on the Galapagos Islands, off the western coast of Ecuador. He was disturbed by the fact that the birds and tortoises of the Galapagos Islands tended to resemble species found on the nearby continent, while inhabits of similar adjoining islands to the Galapagos had quite different animal populations. In London Darwin later learned that the finches he had brought back belonged to a different species, not merely different varieties, as he had originally believed.

FACT FILE

When Charles Darwin first published his theories on evolution they created a sensation, but it took a while before they were accepted.

WHEN DID DARWIN PUBLISH *ON THE ORIGIN OF SPECIES?*

A Galapagos-dwelling tortoise

Upon his return from the voyage, Darwin turned over all the specimens he had brought back to cataloguing experts in Cambridge and London. In South America he had found fossils of extinct armadillos that were similar but not identical to the living animals he had seen. On November 24, 1859 Darwin published his theories in a book called *On The Origin of Species*. It caused a great sensation, but it was some time before it was accepted by the scientific world. The first edition sold out immediately and by 1872 the work had run through six editions. It became generally accepted that evolution took place along the lines that Darwin suggested. His theory on evolution of species solved many puzzles.

FACT FILE

We can see how evolution has changed living things by examining fossils. Fossils preserve the body parts of living creatures from long ago so that we can see how they have changed over millions of years.

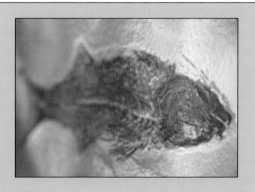

Carl Linnaeus

WHEN DID LINNAEUS DEVELOP THE CLASSIFICATION SYSTEM?

Carl Linnaeus (1707–1778) was a Swedish botanist and explorer who was the first to create a uniform system for naming plants and animals. Most plants and animals have popular names that vary from place to place. Scientific names are given so that the same name is recognized everywhere. Latin is the language used for scientific names. The scientific names are in two parts. The first is the generic name, which describes a group of related living things, and the second name is the specific name, which applies only to that living thing.

FACT FILE

The Latin name of the White Water Lily is *Nymphaea alba*. They are one of a group of plants whose flowers close up for the night.

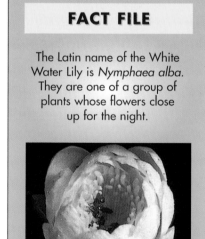

WHEN IS AN ANIMAL TERMED A VERTEBRATE?

An animal is classed as a vertebrate when it has a backbone to provide support for the muscles and protection for the spinal cord. Vertebrates include fish, amphibians, reptiles, birds and mammals. The backbone is actually a series of small bones called vertebrae. They are joined together and locked with rope-like ligaments to provide a flexible but extremely strong anchor for the back muscles. The spinal cord runs down a channel inside the vertebrae, providing protection from damage. Some primitive fish, such as sharks and rays, have a spine made of a tough rubbery material called cartilage. There are approximately 45,000 living species of vertebrates. In size, they range from minute fishes to elephants and whales (of up to 100 tons), the largest animals ever to have existed. They are adapted to life underground, on the surface, and in the air.

FACT FILE

The duck-billed platypus is a very unusual, small, semiaquatic mammal. It lives in lakes and streams of eastern Australia and Tasmania. It is notable in having a broad, flat, rubbery snout, webbed feet, and in that it lays eggs.

WHEN DO BIRDS MIGRATE?

Migration is the mass movement of groups of animals or birds. It is caused by the need to find food, by climatic changes during the year, and by the need to breed. Every autumn, for example, swallows gather in large flocks to rest before they begin their long migration to Africa. Swallows, and their relatives, swifts and martins, all migrate to Africa when the weather becomes too cold for them to catch their insect prey. They return in the spring when the weather in northern Europe begins to warm up. The Arctic tern makes the longest-known migration of any bird we know, by travelling from the Arctic to the Antarctic and then back again. On its flight it passes through Japan, Alaska, Canada and Fiji before returning home again to breed.

FACT FILE

Many fish migrate in both fresh water and the ocean. Tuna make some of the longest migrations. The need to migrate is due to sea temperature, as fish need the correct temperature in order to breed.

WHEN DOES A CYGNET BECOME A SWAN?

FACT FILE

In captivity geese and swans have been known to live for more than 30 years; there are reports of geese exceeding 40 years of age. With luck and cunning a wild swan may survive for 15 to 20 years.

Young swans, or cygnets, are hatched with a complete covering of down and can take to the water as soon as they leave the nest, within 24 to 48 hours. Right from the beginning they can forage for themselves, but at least one parent remains with them, guarding, guiding and, initially, brooding them at night. The dark downy plumage is retained for two to six weeks and is then replaced gradually by the juvenile feathers. The flight feathers are the last to develop, taking from five weeks to as many months. By the age of six months the cygnets are practically indistinguishable from adults in plumage and in size.

WHEN DO ANIMALS BECOME EXTINCT?

GIANT PANDA: less than 1,000 remaining

YELLOW-EYED PENGUIN: about 3,000 left in the wild

RED WOLF: only 200 exist in captivity, none in the wild

According to the theory of evolution, some animal species become extinct because they are less successful than other species that gradually replace them.

These so-called 'failed' animals are also unable to adapt to changing circumstances. Humans have speeded up their extinction by changing the environment so rapidly that animals do not have the time to adapt. For example, the destruction of Indonesian rainforests has left nowhere for the orang-utan to live. It would take millions of years for the animal to evolve into a ground-living creature. Hunting is the main reason for the reduced numbers and probable extinction of animals such as the tiger, the blue whale, and the giant panda.

FACT FILE

The black rhino has been reduced down to about 2,550 due to poaching. Most of the ones that survive today live in protected game parks.

WHEN DO AMPHIBIANS LEAVE THE WATER?

Although frogs and toads can live on land, they have to return to the water to breed. Common frogs can be found in many freshwater habitats. They often show up in garden ponds but are just as happy in lakes, canals and pools. Toads usually prefer wooded ponds and lakes and can sometimes be seen in boggy pools.

Frogs and toads are amphibians, which means they are equally at home on land and water. Toads, however, generally spend more time away from water than most frogs. Their skin is leathery and warty and they do not lose water so easily on dry land. On land a frog hops to escape danger, whereas a toad will walk. The bodies of some frogs and toads have adapted to survive in very dry conditions, such as in deserts.

FACT FILE

A frog's eyes are on top of its head so it can see above the water's surface. This way he can keep a watch out for predators.

115

WHEN DID THE FIRST PLANTS APPEAR?

Plants are organisms that use light as a source of energy and to produce the food they need in order to live and grow. The Earth's original atmosphere contained poisonous gases. The lack of oxygen meant that no animals or plants could survive on the Earth. The earliest plants or plant-like bacteria began the process of photosynthesis, which releases oxygen as well as a waste product. This gas gradually built up in the atmosphere as the plant life spread, making it possible for oxygen-dependent animals to evolve.

Coral was formed by bacteria in much the same way as plants. It is made up of a variety of invertebrate marine organisms of a stonelike, horny, or leathery consistency. They live in colonies begun by just one polyp. Each polyp builds a hard skeleton around itself.

FACT FILE

Lichens are a mixture of algae and fungi. Many grow like a mat over rocks or tree trunks, while others look like a small branched plant.

Coral reef

WHEN DO TREES STOP GROWING?

Californian giant redwood

The simple answer to this question is that trees never stop growing. Trees are the largest living organisms on Earth. The largest tree of all is the Californian giant redwood which can grow nearly 100m high and can have a trunk that is 11 metres thick. The oldest-known trees are bristlecone pine trees. They grow in the White Mountains in California, in the USA. Although they are quite small, some of these gnarled trees are more than 4,500 years old.

Environmental factors such as water availability, soil quality, and change in the weather can affect the growth of a tree. Water is pulled up from the roots to the top of the tree by their leaves.

FACT FILE

Bonsai trees are decorative miniature trees that were first developed in Japan. They are grown in shallow dishes and the shoots and roots are carefully trimmed to stunt their growth. They can live for hundreds of years.

WHEN ARE SEEDS FORMED?

Seeds are the main means by which flowering plants reproduce and spread. After the plant has been fertilized the egg cells develop into a seed from which a new plant can develop. The seed contains an embryo from which the new plant will grow. It also contains a food store to nourish the embryo until it has developed roots and leaves. The seed is enclosed in a tough outer coating to protect it from drying out. Many seeds can be carried by the wind. Some even have a fluffy umbrella like the dandelion seed head (*above*), which enables them to be carried for very long distances.

FACT FILE

The biggest seed is the coco de mer, a kind of coconut that grows in the Seychelles, a group of islands in the Indian Ocean. The coco de mer seeds weigh 250 kg each.

WHEN DOES POLLINATION TAKE PLACE?

FACT FILE

The flowers of orchids are highly specialized for pollination by insects. When the insect pushes into the flower to reach the nectar, the pollinia stick onto its head.

Pollination is the process of transferring pollen from the stamen to stigma. It is possible for flowers to pollinate themselves, or other flowers on the same plant – this is called self-pollination. It is, however, much better for the health of the species if cross-pollination occurs, i.e. pollen is transferred from one plant to another. The most common method involves insects that are attracted to the flowers for their nectar. Pollen grains stick to the insects' bodies and are effectively transferred from one plant to another as the insect moves from flower to flower. Other, less attractive types of flower, use wind to transport their pollen.

TELL ME WHEN : THE NATURAL WORLD

WHEN DO TREES LOSE THEIR LEAVES?

A tree that loses its leaves in winter is called a deciduous tree. Trees that are about to lose their leaves in the autumn conserve their food supplies by withdrawing all the nutrients from the leaves. Chlorophyll is broken down in the leaves, causing their pigment to change. Eventually all the nutrients are moved from the leaves and they wither, turn brown and eventually fall from the tree.

FACT FILE

Every year a tree grows, it deposits a new layer of cells on the outside of its trunk, beneath the bark. This new layer is called an annual ring. By counting the annual rings it is simple to work out the exact age of a tree.

WHEN DO PLANTS EAT INSECTS?

Venus Flytrap

FACT FILE

Some insects use camouflage to blend into their environment, protecting themselves from predators.

Plants growing in bogs and peaty areas often need to supplement their food supply by catching insects. Bog water contains very little nitrogen, but some bog plants can obtain this substance by catching and digesting insects. They are known as insectivorous plants. Other insectivorous plants are covered with sticky tentacles that trap flies. The most remarkable is the Venus flytrap plant. It has two clawed plates that slam together when a fly walks over them and touches a trigger hair. Other insect-eating plants are aquatic, catching tiny crustaceans in bladder-shaped underwater traps. Some of the largest insectivorous plants live in the tropical rainforests.

WHEN DO CATERPILLARS TURN INTO BUTTERFLIES?

Young insects develop in two main ways. Butterflies, bees and beetles, go through a process called metamorphosis. This means that their eggs hatch into larvae or caterpillars. Later these become a pupa or chrysalis, within which an imago, or an adult insect, develops. The larvae may live in a different habitat from the adult and require different foods.

In species such as grasshoppers and locusts, the young that hatch from eggs look rather like small adults, and are called nymphs. As they grow, the nymphs shed their skins, looking more and more like adults each time.

FACT FILE

The wings of a bee or wasp can beat as many as 250 times per second during flight. The wings of midges can beat as many as 1,000 times per second – which accounts for the high-pitched whine that these tiny insects make.

WHEN DO DRAGONFLIES EAT?

Dragonflies are impressive insects with two pairs of powerful clear wings which enable them to catch insects on the wing. They have large eyes for spotting their prey. Dragonfly nymphs live in water and so the adults are usually seen near ponds, rivers and lakes. Some species have a feeding territory which they guard from other dragonflies – their clattering wings can sometimes be heard as they battle. When they mate, most species fly around in tandem before they lay their eggs

Male Emperor dragonfly

in the water or among the waterside vegetation. Dragonfly nymphs are active carnivores. They feed on other insects, but can catch tadpoles or even small fish. On the underside of the head is a flap called the mask. This is armed with sharp jaws and fangs. At rest it is folded, but it can shoot out to catch its prey.

Broad-bodied Libellula

FACT FILE

A dragonfly's eyes are large and give it almost all-around vision. They are sensitive to the slightest movement around them. If you look closely you will be able to see the individual facets of the eye. Each one contains its own lens; together they help form the image seen.

WHEN DO BEES MAKE HONEY?

Bees constantly make honey because it serves them as food. So the whole process of making honey is a way of storing up food for the bee colony. The first thing a bee does is visit flowers and drink the nectar. Then it carries the nectar home in the honey sac. This is a baglike enlargement of the digestive tract just in front of the bee's stomach. There is a valve that separates this section from the stomach.

   The first step in the making of the honey takes place while the nectar is in the bee's honey sac. The sugars found in the nectar undergo a chemical change. The next step is to remove a large part of the water from the nectar. This is done by evaporation, which takes place because of the heat of the hive, and by ventilation. Honey stored in the honeycombs by honeybees has so much water removed from the original nectar that it will keep almost forever! The honey is put into honeycombs to ripen, and to serve as the future food supply for the colony. Honeys differ in taste and appearance, depending on the source of the nectar.

FACT FILE

Honey is removed from the hive by various methods. It may be squeezed from the comb by presses, or it may be sold in the combs cut from the hive. Most honey, however, is removed from the combs by a machine known as 'a honey extractor'.

WHEN DO GLOW WORMS GLOW?

The glow worm is not really a worm at all. It is a firefly in an early stage of development called the larval stage. Most adult fireflies never eat because they did all their eating when they were larvae. They hide during the daytime among the vegetation. After dark, the female climbs up plant stems and the top of her abdomen glows. The light from a larva's glowing body attracts tiny flies and mosquitoes for the larva to eat.

FACT FILE

Woodworm, the larvae of the furniture beetle, cause lots of damage to timber both in buildings and in the wild. The damage is evident from the holes they leave behind.

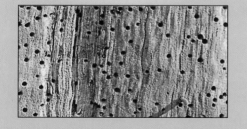

The Waitomo Caves in New Zealand house a memorable type of glow worm. Tourists entering the Glowworm Grotto in small boats see thousands of lights on the cave ceiling. The glow worms look like stars in a night sky. If you cough or use a camera flash, the lights instantly go off. But wait quietly for a few minutes and they flicker back on, until the cave-ceiling 'sky' is again filled with 'stars'.

WHEN DO WATER-DWELLING INSECTS BREATHE?

The saucer bug

Water bugs are found in all sorts of different types of freshwater habitats. They all breathe air and have to return to the surface of the water from time to time. Ponds and lakes are the best habitats for water bugs. Only a few species live in streams and rivers, except where the current is slow-flowing.

Adult water beetles have to breathe air. They do not have gills. Many have a supply of air

beneath their wing cases or under the body which they renew from time to time. Watch a beetle in a tank. Some species come to the surface tail-first, while a few come to the surface head first. Count the number of times a beetle will visit the surface in an hour.

Adult water beetle

FACT FILE

Place a needle on a piece of paper in some water. As the paper sinks, the needle floats, showing surface tension. This same process allows the water boatman to 'walk' on water. It uses its legs like oars to swim.

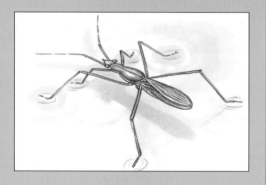

WHEN DO DESERT-DWELLING PLANTS GET WATER?

Plants living in very dry regions are specially adapted to stop them from losing too much water. They have smaller leaves, which are often thin and spiny, or they may have no leaves at all, as in the case of the cacti. Because they have no leaves photosynthesis takes place in the swollen barrel-like stems, which are often covered with protective spines.

Desert plants also conserve water by having a thick waxy coat over their leaves and stems, and by storing water after the rain. Some desert plants have fat, swollen leaves or stems that are filled with water. Desert plants also have extremely long roots that burrow deep into the soil.

FACT FILE

Because plants need to store food and water over the winter, or in dry conditions, underground storage organs develop from roots, stems or leaf bases. We use many of these organs for food.

WHEN IS THE BEST TIME TO SEE AN OWL?

Owls are thick-set, rounded birds with large, flat or rounded heads and legs. Owls are difficult to see because they really come to life at night, and its whole body is especially suited to this kind of life. Once the owl has startled its prey and heard its movement, it can even see it in the dark. This is because the eyeballs of the owl are elastic. It can focus them instantly for any distance. The owl can also open the pupil of its eye very wide. This enables it to make use of all the night light there is. The owl's eyes are placed so that it has to turn its whole head to change the direction of its glance. Even the owl's feathers help it to hunt for its food. The feathers are so soft that the owl can fly noiselessly and thus swoop right down on to its prey.

FACT FILE

Some owls are helpful to farmers because they destroy rats, insects, and other enemies of crops. But there are owls that are fond of chickens and other domestic fowl, and these owls cost the farmer a lot of money.

WHEN DO WOODPECKERS PECK WOOD?

FACT FILE

Most woodpeckers eat insects, but some feed on fruits and berries, and sapsuckers regularly feed on sap from certain trees in some seasons.

There are few birds that are so specialised as the woodpecker. These birds are rarely seen away from the trees that they need to supply their food and nest sites. They are particularly noted for their habit of probing for insects in tree bark and chiselling nest holes in dead wood.

Most woodpeckers spend their entire lives in trees, spiralling up the tree trunks in search of insects. In the spring you can hear the loud calls of woodpeckers, often accompanied by drumming on hollow wood or occasionally on metal. These are the sounds that

are associated with the males marking their territories. Most woodpeckers tend to be rather solitary or travel in pairs.

The green woodpecker's tongue is long and sticky, with a barbed point. It probes into anthills and the ants are dragged out and swallowed. When not being used the tongue winds back, liked a coiled spring, into a groove under the top of the woodpecker's skull.

Green Woodpecker

129

WHEN DO PONDS AND LAKES BECOME POLLUTED?

FACT FILE

Frogs produce large quantities of spawn in the spring. Keep a small amount in a jar with pond weeds and watch it grow into tadpoles.

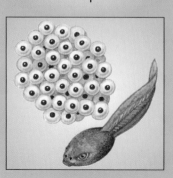

Many years ago the greatest threat to areas of standing water, such as ponds and lakes, was neglect. They gradually filled in and were occupied by shrubs and trees. Today, however, pollution from the modern world is the most serious threat to all water life. Farming practices pollute the water with fertilizers and pesticides. Sewage and waste from industry is also discharged into the rivers. On top of this, rivers and canals are often used as unofficial dumping sites for household waste. One of the saddest sights is to see dead fish floating on top of the water. Hopefully, tough laws controlling pollution may make this a thing of the past.

WHEN DOES PHOTOSYNTHESIS OCCUR?

Photosynthesis is the process by which green plants and certain other organisms transform light energy into chemical energy. During photosynthesis in green plants, light energy is captured and used to convert water, carbon dioxide, and minerals into oxygen and energy-rich organic compounds.

The plant contains packets of a green pigment called chlorophyll that carries out this process. During photosynthesis water and carbon dioxide from the air are converted into sugars that nourish the plant. At the same time the plant releases oxygen into the air.

FACT FILE

The process of photosynthesis takes place mostly in the leaves of a plant. Leaves are large and flattened so that a large area is exposed to sunlight.

carbon dioxide from the air

light energy from the sun

oxygen given off

water and nutrients taken in from the soil

WHEN IS THE BEST TIME TO SEE A BAT?

FACT FILE

A bat called the pipistrelle has adapted to warm cavity walls or hanging tiles in our homes as their normal woodland habitat has been lost and natural roosts have become scarce.

Bats are most easily spotted on open ground near ponds and rivers at dusk. Insects hatch and fly from the water in large numbers, which attracts the bats. The bats catch the insects by a process known as echolocation. This is a technique in which an animal processes sounds and listens for the echoes reflected from surfaces and objects in the environment. From the information contained in these echoes, the animal is able to perceive the objects and work out exactly where they are. Bats change their roosting places from season to season. They choose caves, old ice houses and trees in which to hibernate. These give a constant temperature just above freezing.

WHEN DO BADGERS LEAVE THEIR SETS?

Badgers have distinctive black and white faces, with broad bodies on powerful short legs. They live in colonies, underground (called sets), throwing out obvious heaps of soil at the entrances to their tunnels. They emerge from their sets at dusk to forage for food. They prefer hilly districts on the borders of woods or thickets with easily worked soils.

They feed on earthworms and other small animals, fruits, cereals, and vegetables, using well-worn paths to their chosen pastures or clearings. Badgers take care to keep their sets warm and clean. Damp bedding is thrown out, and fresh, dry grass or straw is scratched up and gathered in armfuls.

FACT FILE

It is fairly easy to spot the entrance to a badger's set as it is much larger than that of a rabbit or fox. The opening to the tunnel has smooth rounded edges, and there is often a musky smell close to it.

WHEN DO HEDGEHOGS ROLL UP INTO A BALL?

FACT FILE

The porcupine is another mammal that uses its spines for defence. Porcupines are heavyset, relatively short-legged rodents, essentially nocturnal and herbivorous in habit.

Although hedgehogs like woodland scrub and cover, as their name suggests, they prefer well cropped or cut grassland to find the worms and insects which are their staple diet. Hedgehogs do not tunnel, but wrap themselves up in dense collections of leaves to form solid hibernation nests under cover, and hide breeding nests in similar places.

Hedgehogs roll themselves up into a ball with spines to protect themselves from most predators. The spines are erect when they roll up, and these form a sharp defence. Born with soft, white ones, dark spines soon grow between these. Fleas, ticks, and lice enjoy life among these spines.

WHEN DO ANIMALS HIBERNATE?

The word 'hibernate' comes from the Latin and means 'winter sleep'. Certain animals hibernate during the winter months to escape the severe weather conditions and because food is hard to find. The sleep of a true hibernator, like the hedgehog, is almost like death and is quite unlike ordinary sleep. The temperature of its body decreases until it is only a little warmer than the air of its den. Because of this, the animal burns the food stored in their bodies very, very slowly. They need less oxygen, and as a result their breathing is slower and their hearts beat only faintly. When spring comes, the animals are awakened by the change in temperature, moisture, and by hunger.

FACT FILE

Many mammals, like the bear, do not really hibernate. They do sleep more in the winter than in the summer, but it is not the deep sleep of hibernation.

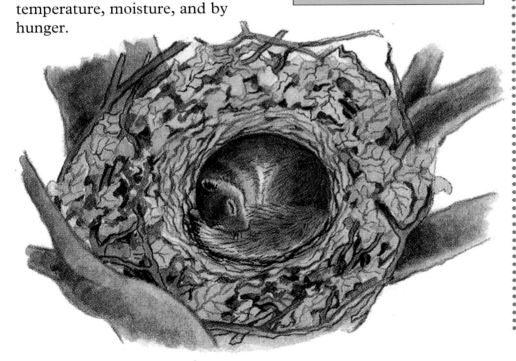

WHEN DO WHITE SEALS TURN DARK?

The common seal can be found on sandy estuaries, fjords and rocky inlets away from the full force of the open sea. Although they live and feed in the water, they still come to the shore to breed and to moult their hair. A seal pup is born with thick white fur but will lose this shortly after it is born and it will be replaced by a much darker, sleeker coat. Their diet includes all kinds of seafoods: fish, shellfish, crabs, and lobsters.

FACT FILE

The pup of a seal will suckle for 10 minutes, five or six times a day. Their birth weight doubles in one week. After a month the pups have grown at an amazing rate, and the mother will then leave to mate with another bull. At this stage the pup enters the sea to fend for itself.

WHEN WILL WHALES BECOME EXTINCT?

Archaeological evidence suggests that primitive whaling by the Inuit and others in the North Atlantic and North Pacific was practised by 3000 BCE. The difference between the small-scale activities of these peoples for food and blubber and commercial whaling in the 20th and 21st centuries is one of scale. All whale species have been threatened by this and by pollution and drift net fishing. The grey whale was hunted almost to extinction by 1925 but like other species has been under international protection since the 1940s. As recently as 2010, the International Whaling Commission extended protection for a minimum of 24 years for many species, because of huge international pressure from concerned individuals. Japan's fishing fleet remains a threat to whale populations.

FACT FILE

The humpback whale was also hunted almost to extinction, and its numbers dropped from 100,000 to 3,000 today. It is now generally protected.

WHEN ARE FUNGI EDIBLE?

Popularly, the term mushroom is used to identify the edible fungi; whereas the term toadstool is often reserved for inedible or poisonous fungi. In a very restricted sense, mushroom indicates the common edible fungus of fields and meadows. Mushrooms have insignificant nutritive value. Their chief worth is as a specialty food of delicate, subtle taste and agreeable texture. Fungi can be found in damp areas, or growing on tree trunks.

Poisoning by wild mushrooms is common and may be fatal or produce merely mild stomach disturbance or slight allergic reaction. It is important that every mushroom intended for eating is accurately identified before you try to eat them.

FACT FILE

Fungi live on organic matter. In the soil, fungi are the most important agent in the breakdown of dead plant and animal material, recycling it so that plants can use the nutrients.

WHEN DO WE SEE FAIRY RINGS?

A fairy ring is a circular pattern that is produced by fungi growing in grassland. As the fungus grows out from a central point it forms a circle, and at the edges of this circle the grass changes in appearance. Meanwhile the original fungus dies off, so all that is left is the

expanding ring of fungus growing beneath the surface. Sometimes a ring of mushrooms also appears. These fairy rings keep growing for many years, perhaps even for centuries. They can reach a very large size unless they are disturbed, for example when the land is ploughed.

FACT FILE

Fungi represent a separate kingdom of living things and should not be regarded as either plants or animals. There are many thousands of different kinds, showing a huge variety of shape and lifestyle. The fungus kingdom is split into two divisions – slime moulds and the true fungi.

HISTORY

AND EVENTS

CONTENTS

WHEN WAS THE STONE AGE?

Stone Age man (known as Neanderthal man) lived in Europe from about 100,000 to 35,000 years ago. They sheltered in caves, made fire and hunted animals using stone tools and wooden spears.

Historians call this period of prehistory the Stone Age, because stone was the most important material used by the first tool-makers. These early stone-crafting techniques show surprising skill. They chipped or flaked off bits of stone to make shaped tools including hand axes and knives. Both the hand axe and scraper were usually made from flint, while spear heads were often shaped from wood or deer antlers.

The Stone Age hunters killed deer and other animals with spears, bows and stones, often ambushing them on the move. Although they were not as fast as the animals they hunted, they made up for it by using teamwork and accuracy with their weapons.

A skull of a Neanderthal man

Spear head

Scraper

Hand axe

FACT FILE

Stone Age people hunted with bows, spears and flint axes. On the American grasslands, groups of hunters drove to extinction large grazing animals such as mastodons and giant bison.

142

WHEN WAS BABYLON FOUNDED?

After the fall of Ur in 2000 BCE, many cities of Mesopotamia were ruled by the Amorites, whose two strongholds were Isin and Larsa. In 1763 BCE, Larsa fell to a great army led by Hammurabi (1792–1750 BCE). The new ruler gave a new name – Babylonia – to the kingdoms of Sumer and Akkad.

The Ishtar Gate, Babylon

The city of Babylon had magnificent temples and palaces. People entered the city through eight great bronze gates. The most magnificent of these was the Ishtar Gate, which was decorated with patterns and pictures of lions, bulls and dragons – all in shiny, patterned bricks.

Babylon's winding, narrow streets were lined with private houses. Most had a courtyard with rooms around it. In the city walls were gates, around which traders held markets. Traders and merchants travelled as far afield as Syria, Assyria and the kingdoms of the Persian Gulf.

The Babylonians produced written records by carving picture symbols onto clay tablets. The tablets carried information about astronomy and mathematics, as well as records of legal and business matters and religious texts.

FACT FILE

The ancient Babylonians were the first to study the stars, some time before 2000 BCE. They knew of five planets: Jupiter, Mars, Mercury, Saturn and Venus.

143

WHEN WAS THE PARTHENON BUILT?

The ancient Greeks were pioneers in medicine, mathematics and science. They looked at the world in the light of logic and reason, and made some fundamental discoveries. In the year 432 BCE a building called the Parthenon was completed. The Parthenon was built in Athens to venerate the city's protector, the goddess Athena. Her gold and ivory decorated statue was inside the great hall, enclosed by columns which supported the roof like a forest of stones.

The Greeks built many beautiful temples to their gods. Stone columns, as used in the Parthenon, were a typical feature of many Greek buildings.

FACT FILE

Greek actors wore masks to show what kind of character (comic or tragic) they played. Audiences would sit in the open air on a hillside to watch the plays.

WHEN WAS HADRIAN'S WALL BUILT?

Hadrian's Wall was built in CE 122 to defend the northern frontier of Roman Britain. It acted as a checkpoint on movement between England and Scotland. The wall took eight years to build and stretches for 118 km (73 mi).

At this time the Roman Empire was governed by the personal will of the emperor, but the emperor's power rested on his army. Weak or bad emperors were sometimes overthrown by army generals. Some emperors ruled well – Hadrian, for example, travelled widely to inspect building projects. Others, such as Nero and Caligula, were cruel or mad. The Romans were such good organizers that the empire usually kept working even when there was a fool at its heart.

FACT FILE

A Roman coin stamped with the head of the Emperor Hadrian. During his reign, he personally visited nearly every province in the Roman Empire.

WHEN WAS THE START OF THE ISLAMIC FAITH?

The Dome of the Rock, Jerusalem

In the first centuries after Christ, Christianity spread from Palestine into North Africa, Asia Minor and across Europe. Further east, many people in the Arabian peninsula were still pagans, worshipping ancient gods. In this region, during the 600s, there arose a new religion called Islam.

Islam had its roots in the Hebrew–Christian belief in one God, and its prophet was Muhammad (CE 570–632). Through Muhammad's perseverance, Mecca became the holiest city of Islam. Muhammad's teachings were written down in the Koran, the holy book of Islam.

FACT FILE

The people of Arabia traded by camel caravans, which broke their journeys at an oasis. Muhammad knew this life well. As a young man he worked as a merchant.

WHEN WAS THE BIGGEST GROWTH OF THE MUSLIM EMPIRE?

The advance of Islam seemed unstoppable in the late 600s. The Byzantine and Persian empires could not halt the armies of Islam, and nor could Egypt. By CE 700 Muslims controlled most of the North African coast and ships patrolled the Mediterranean Sea and Indian Ocean. Muslims from Morocco invaded Spain, but the advance of Islam into western Europe was stopped in CE 732 by the Frankish army of Charles Martel.

Under the Ummayad family rule there were four classes of citizens: Arabian Muslims; new converts; Christians, Jews and Mandaens (a Persian sect); and slaves. The new converts included people from Egypt, Syria, Persia and Asia Minor. They adopted Arab ways, but brought to the Arabs a wealth of new learning in philosophy, medicine, art and science.

A scene from 'The Thousand and One Nights'

147

WHEN WAS THE START OF SAXON BRITAIN?

FACT FILE

Treasures unearthed from a burial site at Sutton Hoo, Suffolk, included a gold belt, a sword and shield, an iron helmet, and several items of jewelllery. Finally there was a sceptre and standard which must have belonged to the dead King Redwald.

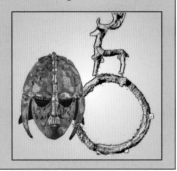

In the late CE 300s the Roman army was hard pressed to fight off waves of barbarian invasions. Troops in distant outposts, such as the British Isles, were needed to defend the empire, and by CE 410 the last Roman soldiers had left England for mainland Europe. Without the Roman army to protect them, the Roman Britons of England were unable to prevent these mercenaries, and any new bands of invaders, from taking over land they wanted. The newcomers were a mixture of people – Angles, Saxons, Jutes, Frisians – who became known as the 'English'. The invaders came to England to find land to farm. They were well armed and tough, and drove away many Britons, who moved into western England.

Saxon farmers

Ships moored beside a Viking town

WHEN DID THE VIKINGS PROGRESS THROUGH EUROPE?

The Vikings came from Scandinavia (Norway, Denmark and Sweden). Their homelands offered little spare farmland for a growing population, so many Vikings went abroad in search of new lands. The Vikings were farmers, but also fierce warriors, and their first impact on western Europe was a violent one. They began to sail across the North Sea in the late CE 700s, raiding the coasts of Britain and mainland Europe. They raided churches and towns, carrying off loot and slaves. Their raids caused panic, and rulers tried to buy off the invaders with gold. This, however, only encouraged the Vikings to come back for more.

FACT FILE

Decorative brooches such as this were used by both Viking men and women to hold their outer garments (cloaks and tunics) in place.

149

A section of the Bayeux Tapestry

ET SAPIENTEAR : EAD PRELIVM :

WHEN WAS THE NORMAN CONQUEST?

FACT FILE

In CE 1085 William I ordered a survey of land in England. The findings were written down in the Domesday Book (Domesday means 'Day of Judgement'). It is the best record we have of life in England at that time.

William of Normandy ruled England from CE 1066 to 1087 He claimed that Edward the Confessor promised him the throne in CE 1051. He also said that Harold (who was shipwrecked in France in CE 1064) had sworn to accept this.

The story of William's invasion and the battle of Hastings on October 14, 1066, is told in 72 scenes in the Bayeux Tapestry. After the crucial battle William declared himself king. The English nobles lost their lands and French became the language of government. William and his barons built castles to guard their new land. A new age was beginning.

William of Normandy

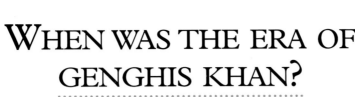

WHEN WAS THE ERA OF GENGHIS KHAN?

Genghis Khan
(1167–1227)

In the year 1167, a child called Temujin was born on the desolate plains of Mongolia. When the boy was nine, his father was murdered and his family was left poor and friendless. From this grim beginning Temujin grew up to become one of the world's greatest conquerors. He was hailed by the Mongols as Genghis Khan – the 'Universal Ruler'.

In 1206, Genghis Khan became leader of all the Mongol people, and began to build his astonishing empire. He was a ruthless warrior, destroying entire cities and their populations during his conquests. Yet he succeeded in keeping the peace.

Genghis Khan died of a fever in 1227, but the Mongols continued to build up the empire.

FACT FILE

The Mongols lived on the flat, grassy steppes of Asia, wandering with their herds of sheep, goats and cattle. They carried their tentlike felt homes, called yurts, around with them. The Mongols were tough and violent, and splendid horse riders.

WHEN WAS THE HUNDRED YEARS' WAR?

The 14th century was filled with wars. The longest and most exhausting of these wars was between England and France. It lasted, on and off, until the middle of the 1400s, and is known as the Hundred Years' War. It actually spanned from 1337 until 1453, by which time the French, inspired by Joan of Arc, had driven the English from Maine, Gascony and Normandy and the war was finally won.

The conflict was a very complicated one. The Plantagenet kings of England also ruled a large part of France, while the rest belonged to the king of France. Both kings wanted to be the sole ruler of a united country.

There were plenty of other reasons for the war. The French supported the Scots in their struggle against England. The English, in turn, claimed the throne of France when Charles IV died in 1328 and left no heirs.

FACT FILE

English troops lay siege to the French town of Troyes. The city gates have been shut and barred against them. English officials are trying to persuade the leaders of Troyes to surrender.

Edward, known as the Black Prince

WHEN DID THE GREAT NATIONS OF EUROPE EMERGE?

After about 1450, the great nations of Europe began to emerge. For most of their history they had consisted of small warring states, or had been invaded by powerful neighbours. Now things were changing fast.

The connection between France and England was broken at last. Spain and Portugal grew stable enough to found their great seagoing empires. Germany (part of the Holy Roman Empire) had strong leaders from the Habsburg dynasty.

The marriage in 1492 of King Ferdinand and Queen Isabella of Spain helped to unite the two strong Christian kingdoms of Aragon and Castile. Ferdinand and Isabella also completed the great 'reconquest' of Spain from Muslim control, which had begun over 400 years earlier.

FACT FILE

Unlike Spain, Italy remained a divided country, split up into several states ruled by different powers. In the north were the wealthy city-states, such as Florence, Milan and Urbino. The crest (below) belongs to the Sforza family, who ruled over Milan.

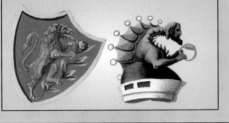

King Ferdinand and Queen Isabella

WHEN WAS THE THIRTY YEARS' WAR?

The last and biggest religious war began in Germany in 1618 and continued until 1648. This very messy conflict became known as the Thirty Years' War.

The war started in a dramatic way. Protestants in Bohemia (now part of the Czech Republic) were angry with their new king, Ferdinand. He was a member of the powerful Spanish Habsburg family, and wanted to restore Bohemia to the Catholic faith. The Protestants banded together and threw some Catholic officials from an upstairs window in Prague Castle. The incident sparked off a civil war in Bohemia. In 1619 the rebels expelled Ferdinand and chose a new king, the Protestant Frederick.

FACT FILE

When the Protestants threw the Catholic officials out of the window of Prague Castle, it became known as the 'Defenestration of Prague'.

WHEN WAS THE CIVIL WAR IN BRITAIN?

In 1603, England had a new king-
James I. He was the first of the Stuart
monarchs and his accession to the English
throne marked the end of the Tudor rule.
James, son of Mary Queen of Scots, was already
James VI of Scotland and wished to unite the
kingdoms of the
British Isles. He
believed in the
divine right of kings
to rule. His reign was
very unpopular in England, but less so
than that of his son Charles I, who came
to the throne in 1625. Charles tried to
rule without parliament and was faced
with a rebellion. He tried, unsuccessfully
to arrest five members of the House of
Commons for treason, and was forced to
flee to London. By August 1642 he had
declared war on the parliamentary
supporters (the 'Roundheads' and the civil
war began.

FACT FILE

A Roundhead helmet. Oliver
Cromwell reorganized the
Roundhead forces into a
professional force known as
the 'New Model Army'.

A combined force of Scots and Roundheads defeated Charles and his Royalist forces at the battle of
Marston Moor, in Yorkshire, in 1644.

Russian peasants working the land

WHEN DID PETER BECOME TSAR OF RUSSIA?

Peter the Great became tsar of Russia in 1696. A violently energetic giant of a man, (over 2 m (6.5 ft) tall), he resolved to use his energy to make Russia a strong and modern state.

The mainly peasant economy had a bloody and unsettled past, and was just starting to emerge as a more stable economy and develop modern methods of farming and industry. Under Peter's rule, this progress increased rapidly.

Peter travelled widely in western Europe, to learn about the latest progressive systems. At home, he modernised the transport system instigating building projects for roads and canals and introduced new methods to mining and industry.

FACT FILE

The beautiful city of St Petersburg lies beside the River Neva. Its magnificent Winter Palace was the winter home of the tsars. As a result of working in the difficult marshy conditions, thousands of peasants died while building Peter the Great's new city.

WHEN WAS AUSTRALIA DISCOVERED?

FACT FILE

In 1776, Cook set sail to find a sea passage from the Pacific round the north of America to the Atlantic. Ice blocked his way. He was the first European to reach Hawaii, where he was killed in 1779.

In 1768, the British government sent an expedition to find the mysterious southern continent. Its leader was James Cook, and his ship was a small but tough vessel called *Endeavour*. After visiting the island of Tahiti, Cooked sailed southwards and then west until he sighted an unknown land. It turned out to be New Zealand. The *Endeavour* sailed on, searching for the east coast of Australia. By 1770 Cook reached the coast of what he knew to be Australia. He followed it northwards until he found a suitable place to land. He called this Botany Bay.

Cook's first meeting with the Maori people of New Zealand in 1769

WHEN WAS THE AMERICAN REVOLUTION?

The American victory over British forces at Saratoga in 1777

By the year 1763 more than two million British colonists were living in North America. Their main ambition was to be able to govern themselves. Britain, however, had different ideas about her colonies, because they were an important market for trade. The British government were concerned about who was going to pay for the forces that were still stationed to protect North America. The answer was the colonists themselves through new and increased taxes.

The Americans had never been taxed before and protested loudly. They had no-one to put their case to the parliament in London, so they took direct action. By 1775 the whole colony was in a state of rebellion. This was the opening of America's struggle for freedom.

FACT FILE

On July 4, 1776, representatives of the 13 colonies signed a Declaration of Independence. This broke off all political connections with Britain.

WHEN WAS THE FRENCH REVOLUTION?

French troops fought alongside American colonists in the American War of Independence. The cost of these wars left France virtually bankrupt. To try to raise money, the French king, Louis XVI, proposed an increase in taxes. However, most of the country's richest people – the clergy and the noblemen – did not pay taxes. So the burden fell on the ordinary peasants. On July 14, 1789, a mob attacked the royal prison in Paris, the Bastille. Although few prisoners were released, this event marked the end of royal power in France and the beginning of the Revolution.

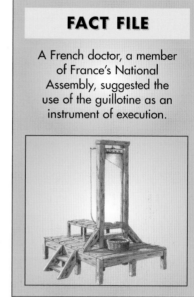

FACT FILE

A French doctor, a member of France's National Assembly, suggested the use of the guillotine as an instrument of execution.

On July 4, 1789, a mob attacked the Bastille, in Paris

WHEN WAS THE INDUSTRIAL REVOLUTION?

The Industrial Revolution, which began in Europe in the early 1700s, saw dramatic improvements in travel and the carrying of cargo.

In Britain, private roads called turnpikes were built in the 1750s and travellers had to pay tolls to use them. But these soon became rutted and in need of repair. In about 1810, a Scottish engineer called John Macadam developed a new type of hard-wearing road surface that drained easily.

As industry expanded, greater loads of heavy goods such as coal and iron had to be taken across country. Rivers did not always go in the right direction, so canals were dug instead. The first modern canal system opened in France in 1681, and was copied later in Britain and the USA. By about 1800, there were nearly 7,000 km of canal in Britain. Steam power was the driving force of the Industrial Revolution. In 1804 an Englishman, Richard Trevithick, built a steam engine which could pull itself along on iron rails. His idea was later developed by George Stephenson, whose locomotive *Rocket*, was used to pull trains from 1829.

FACT FILE

In 1837 the English engineer Isambard Kingdom Brunel launched the Great Western, the first all-steam ship to carry passengers across the Atlantic.

A paddlewheel from Brunel's *Great Western*

WHEN WAS THE SLAVE TRADE ABOLISHED IN AFRICA?

During the 1700s the slave trade brought misery to thousands of Africans, who were transported across the Atlantic Ocean and forced to work as slaves on plantations in the Americas. This trade also brought huge wealth to those who ran it – the shipbuilders, shipowners, merchants and traders.

Many people began to condemn the slave trade and to call for it to be abolished. The slave trade came to an end in the British Empire in 1807 and was finally abolished within the empire in 1833. Slavery continued elsewhere, however. It did not come to an end in the United States until after the American Civil War in 1865, and continued in Brazil until 1889.

In 1788 an association was formed in London to encourage British exploration and trade in Africa. Many British explorers set out to explore Africa along its rivers. Probably the most famous of all the expeditions was led by David Livingstone, who set out to look for the source of the River Nile. After being out of contact for almost three years, he was eventually found by the American journalist Henry Stanley.

David Livingstone

A typical colonists' hat

FACT FILE

The anti-slavery movement was strongest in Britain and the USA. Many abolitionist speakers joined the struggle to gain equal rights for black people.

WHEN WERE THE OPIUM WARS?

The Manchus ruled China for more than 250 years, from 1644 until 1912. This time is known as the Qing dynasty. In the early 1800s, British merchants started to trade opium illegally from India to China. Despite the fact that the addictive dangers of opium were well known, the British government backed the merchants. They wanted to force China to accept more open trade.

The first Opium War broke out in 1839, and was started when Chinese officials seized 20,000 chests of opium in Guangzhou. It ended with the Treaty of Nanjing in 1842. Under the terms of this treaty, Hong Kong became a British colony and more Chinese ports were opened up to European trade. A second Opium War (1856 to 1860) extended the trading rights of European nations in China. Under Manchu rule, all Chinese males had to follow the tradition of wearing their hair in a pigtail. It was seen as a sign of loyalty to the Qing dynasty.

FACT FILE

The skyline of modern Hong Kong. The island of Hong Kong came under British control in 1842, and Britain later gained part of the nearby Kowloon Peninsula. Control of Hong Kong passed back to the Chinese government in 1997.

WHEN WAS THE RUSSIAN REVOLUTION?

The last tsar, Nicholas II, ruled from 1894 until his abdication in 1917. In the early years of his reign there was increasing discontent amongst ordinary Russians. Many people, including the Bolshevik leader Vladimir Illyich Lenin, followed the teachings of Karl Marx, the founder of communism. In 1905 this discontent boiled over when troops fired on thousands of striking workers outside the tsar's Winter Palace in St Petersburg. The rebellion was quickly put down, but hundreds of workers were killed and wounded.

In early 1917 riots broke out again and this time the troops supported the rioters. Nicholas II abdicated, and a provisional government was put in place.

FACT FILE

Nicholas II and his family. Imprisoned by the Bolsheviks in 1917, they were most probably shot the following year.

WHEN DID THE FIRST SETTLERS ARRIVE IN AUSTRALIA?

Commemorative Australian stamps of Cook's arrival in Botany Bay

In April 1770, Captain James Cook had sailed along the east coast of Australia. He and his crew had landed at a place called Botany Bay and claimed the land for Britain, naming the region New South Wales.

Eighteen years later, in 1788, the first ships full of settlers arrived from Britain. These settlers were all convicts, transported from Britain for their various crimes. Under the command of Captain Arthur Philip, the convicts were set to work founding a penal colony in Botany Bay. About 300,000 Aborigines were living in Australia when the settlers first arrived from Europe. They were divided into about 500 tribal groups.

FACT FILE

Convicts were to be transported to Australia and confined in prison ships like this one. By 1830 about 58,000 convicts had come to Australia. Many were more or less habitual urban thieves, some political, while a substantial proportion were Irish.

German soldiers in trenches along the Western Front

WHEN DID WORLD WAR I BEGIN?

FACT FILE

A British soldier from World War I. Typically, soldiers would spend a week or more in a front-line trench before going back to their dugout in a support trench.

As the 19th century drew to a close, there was an increase in rivalry between the different nations of Europe. They competed against each other for control of colonies, and for industrial and military power. In 1882, Germany, Austria–Hungary and Italy (known as the Central Powers) formed an alliance called the Triple Alliance, promising to protect each other in the event of an attack. In 1904, Britain joined with France in a similar alliance. They were joined by Russia in 1907 to form the Triple Entente. Europe was finally plunged into war by the action of an assassin in the Bosnian city of Sarajevo in 1914. Soon all the major European powers were drawn into conflict. Russia, backed by France, supported Serbia. Then Germany invaded neutral Belgium and attacked France, drawing Britain into the conflict.

WHEN WAS THE WALL STREET CRASH?

In the late 1920s, the price of shares on the New York Stock Exchange increased rapidly. More and more people bought stocks and shares in the hope of selling them again when their price had gone up – therefore making a large profit. When prices dropped in October 1929, people rushed to sell their stocks and shares before it was too late, but prices fell even further.

This event is known as the Wall Street Crash. Thousands of people lost all their money, many businesses and banks shut down and unemployment soared.

FACT FILE

During the worst years of the Depression, many people were forced to rely on charity and government hand-outs for their most basic needs. In 1932 Franklin D. Roosevelt was elected US present. His 'New Deal' aimed to create jobs and to protect people's savings by regulating banks more closely.

The Stock Exchange at the time of the collapse

WHEN WAS THE RISE OF FASCISM IN EUROPE?

Many people hoped that World War I was the 'war to end all wars'. However, during the 1920s and 1930s there were a lot of political changes in many countries. In 1922 these changes led to the growth of the Fascist movement. ('Fascism' comes from the word *fasces*, meaning a bundle of branches.) Fascism promised strong leadership and to restore the national economy and pride. This was a very powerful message in the years of the Great Depression, and many people in Europe supported the various Fascist parties.

Italy was the first country to have a Fascist ruler. In 1922, Benito Mussolini marched to Rome and demanded that the Italian king, Victor Emmanuel III, make him Prime Minister.

FACT FILE

Oswald Mosley set up the British Union of Fascists after a visit to Italy in 1932. His supporters were known as 'the Blackshirts'.

WHEN WAS WORLD WAR II?

Adolph Hitler

In March 1939, the German leader Adolph Hitler threatened to invade Poland. Hitler had already shown the seriousness of his intentions by taking over Austria (in 1938) and Czechoslovakia (in 1939). Both Great Britain and France gave guarantees to help Poland if it was attacked. So when Hitler invaded Poland on September 1, 1939, Britain and France were forced to declare war on Germany.

Under Hitler's leadership, Germany had been well prepared for war. During 1939 and 1940, German troops scored victories in Poland, Denmark, Norway, Belgium, the Netherlands and France. Before the war started, Hitler had signed a 'non-aggression pact' with the Soviet Union, both sides promising not to attack the other. As German troops swept across Europe, Soviet troops attacked Estonia, Latvia, Lithuania and Finland. World War II ended in 1945.

FACT FILE

Winston Churchill was Britain's wartime leader from May 1940 until just before the war ended. Here he is seen making his famous 'V for victory' sign.

A standard World War II helmet

WHEN WAS THE BOMBING OF PEARL HARBOR?

On 7 December, 1941, there was a surprise attack by the Japanese airforce on the United States navy base at Pearl Harbor in Hawaii. Although the attack crippled the US Navy in the Pacific Ocean, it also drew the Americans into World War II. The USA and their Allies declared war on Japan on December 8, 1941. Japan joined Germany and Italy to form the Axis alliance.

During the summer of 1942, US forces successfully halted the Japanese advance at the battles of Midway Island, Guadalcanal and Coral Sea. After Pearl Harbor, however, Japanese forces quickly took control of much of Southeast Asia, including Singapore, Burma and the Philippines.

FACT FILE

On the morning of 6 June, 1944, thousands of Allied troops went ashore along the coast of Normandy in northern France, in what became known as the D-Day landings.

WHEN WAS THE FIRST ATOMIC BOMB EXPLOSION?

Technological advances in the machines and weapons of war were rapid during the 20th century. During World War I, inventions included the tank and the fighter aircraft. At sea, one of the major advances in military marine technology happened before the war, with the building of the battleship *Dreadnought*.

During World War II, the Germans began a new type of heavily armed warfare: *Blitzkrieg* or lightning war. But ultimately, the most significant and horrific development in modern warfare came with the invention of the atomic bomb in the USA. The first atomic bomb was exploded in an experiment in New Mexico, USA in July 1945. In August 1945, the USA effectively brought the war against Japan to a catastrophic end when it dropped two atomic bombs on the Japanese cities of Nagasaki and Hiroshima. An estimated 130,000 people were killed and many more suffered terrible after effects.

FACT FILE

Both the British and the French armies experimented with tanks during World War I. These armoured vehicles were first used to effect at the Battle of Cambrai in 1917.

WHEN DID INDIA GAIN INDEPENDENCE?

FACT FILE

Mohandas Gandhi was known as Mahatma Gandhi. He was assassinated in 1948, at the end of India's long struggle for independence.

Many Indians wanted independence from British rule, and a chance to build up industry and wealth in India itself. By the end of World War II it was clear that Britain could no longer ignore the demands of the Indian people. But negotiations were complicated by the demands of Muslims in India. Violence broke out between Hindus and Muslims, and Indians and British leaders eventually agreed to divide India into the two states of Hindu India and Muslim Pakistan.

India gained its independence in August 1947. Millions of Hindus and Muslims fled from their homes. As people tried to move to their new homes, hundreds of thousands of them were killed.

171

WHEN WAS THE COLD WAR?

After World War II, the United States and the USSR emerged as the two main powers in the world – known as 'superpowers'. Although they had fought together to defeat Nazi Germany, differences between the two superpowers soon led to the start of the 'Cold War'.

The Cold War started in August 1945, and it was a political war between the USSR and its communist allies, and the USA and other non-communist countries. It did not involve any fighting, although there was a threat of military action on several occasions.

FACT FILE

Mikhail Gorbachev introduced political, social and economic reform, known as *perestroika*, when he came to power in Russia.

Allied leaders at the Yalta Conference

WHEN WAS THE BERLIN WALL DEMOLISHED?

In August 1961, the German Democratic Republic began under the leadership of Erich Honecker to block off East Berlin and the GDR from West Berlin by means of barbed wire and antitank obstacles. Streets were torn up and barricades of paving stones were erected. Tanks gathered at crucial places. The subway and local railway services between East and West Berlin were interrupted. Inhabitants of East Berlin and the GDR were no longer allowed to enter the West. In the following days, construction brigades began replacing the temporary barriers with a solid wall, which stood in place for nearly 30 years. In November 1989, after weeks of discussion about new travel laws, the Berlin Wall was demolished.

FACT FILE

With the end of communist rule in the USSR, many of the symbols of communism, for example statues of former leaders such as Lenin, were dismantled.

GENERAL

KNOWLEDGE

CONTENTS

WHEN WAS COFFEE FIRST BREWED?

An interesting fact about the use of coffee is that it was first enjoyed without even being brewed. East African tribes have used the fruit of the coffee tree for centuries as an item of food. They would roast the berries in an open pan or prepare them with animal fat, and then eat them.

The first coffee plants probably grew in Kaffa, a province of Ethiopia. This province may have given coffee its name. In the 14th century Arabian merchants came to Kaffa and became acquainted with the coffee seeds. They then began to cultivate coffee in the Yemen. This is where the people began to brew coffee. The followers of Mohammad were forbidden to drink wine, and coffee was a stimulating beverage that could take the place of wine for them.

About the middle of the 15th century, the use of coffee as a beverage spread from Yemen to Mecca, and from there to Baghdad, Cairo, Damascus and other places. There were coffee houses in Cairo as early as 1511. Coffee was first introduced to Western Europe around 1615.

FACT FILE

Tea is another popular beverage. The Chinese are the original and greatest tea drinkers. They have enjoyed tea for more than 4,000 years. It was only about 300 years ago that Europeans first tasted tea.

WHEN WERE COINS FIRST MADE?

FACT FILE

The first coins in America were struck by the English in 1652. They were the New England shillings, and were crude coins about the size of a quarter.

The first coins were made in the seventh century BCE by the Lydians. They were a wealthy and powerful people living in Asia Minor. These primitive coins were made of 'electrum', which is a natural composition of 75 per cent gold and 25 per cent silver. They were about the size and shape of a bean and were known as 'staters' or 'standards'.

The Greeks saw these coins and appreciated the usefulness of a standard metal money, so they began to make coins too. Gold coins were the most valuable and next came silver and finally copper.

A selection of coins

WHEN WAS THE FIRST FURNITURE USED?

The first record we have of furniture as we think of it today comes from the Egyptians. At least 4,000 years ago they were using chairs, tables, stools and chests. Some of the chairs had high backs and arms, decorated with carved animals' heads. Others were simple square stools with crossed legs which folded together like camp chairs. Egyptian beds were only a framework, often very low. The Egyptians did not use pillows on their beds. They used headrests of wood and ivory.

The Babylonians and Assyrians also had elaborate furniture. Kings and queens rested on high couches with footstools, or sat in high-backed chairs while they ate from high stands and tables.

FACT FILE

Romans liked to fill their houses with objects for decoration, so they needed many kinds of furniture. They used carved and painted wooden chests. They also developed the cupboard.

WHEN WAS THE UMBRELLA INVENTED?

In the twenty-first century, it seems natural that we put up an umbrella to keep us from getting wet when it rains. But originally, the umbrella was invented as a shade against the sun not a protection from rain. It is not certain who invented the umbrella, but we have evidence to suggest that the Chinese first used it in ancient times, as early as the eleventh century BCE. We know that umbrellas featured in the form of sunshades, in ancient Egypt and Babylon, and that, curiously, it came to represent power and authority. In the Far East, in those days, the umbrella could only be used by royalty and those in high office. It would seem that the Greeks were the first to use the umbrella in Europe, once again, as protection against the sun. It is said that the first in Europe to use umbrellas to protect them from the rain were the ancient Romans.

During the Middle Ages, the umbrella practically disappeared, only to re-emerge in Italy in the late sixteenth century. By 1680, the umbrella was seen in France, and later in England. By the eighteenth century the umbrella was used as protection against rain throughout most of Europe.

FACT FILE

Following the invention of plastic other ways of protecting yourself from the rain are available, for example this raincoat with hood.

179

WHEN WAS THE CROSSWORD PUZZLE INVENTED?

The crossword puzzle is both a new thing and a not-so-new thing. Since ancient times there was a word square. In a word square the letters spelled the same words horizontally and vertically.

The crossword is built on a pattern of black and white squares, with different words interlocking across and down. There are numbered definitions given as clues to the words. So the crossword puzzle added some new things.

The very first crossword puzzle was put together by a man called Arthur Winn. It first appeared in a Sunday supplement of the New York *World* on December 21, 1913. It remained as a feature of this newspaper for some time.

¹P	A	²R	R	O	³T	⁴T	
A		E		⁵R	O	E	⁶E
⁷C	A	S	E	D			N
K		T		I			D
E		⁸O		N	C		E
⁹T	A	R		A			A
	¹⁰S	E	L	L	E	R	

In 1924 the first book of crossword puzzles appeared. Up until that time, the crossword puzzle had not been very popular. But after this, it became a nationwide craze.

FACT FILE

Another type of puzzle which is very popular is the jigsaw puzzle. This is a picture which is printed onto card and then cut into many pieces. These pieces interlock so that you can recreate the picture.

WHEN WERE THE FIRST SKYSCRAPERS BUILT?

FACT FILE

For hundreds of years cathedrals stood as the tallest structures in the world. Tall spires were added to give greater height.

All over the world today, wherever big cities have grown up, there are very tall buildings that might be called skyscrapers. There is no special reason for calling a building a skyscraper, it is simply a name we have given to very tall buildings. In the nineteenth century, as cities grew more crowded, the value of land rose. In order to make room for more offices on a small plot of land, it was necessary to erect taller buildings. The first skyscraper in the United States was the Home Insurance Building in Chicago, which was designed in 1883.

WHEN WAS THE TAJ MAHAL BUILT?

The story of the Taj Mahal is in fact a sad and beautiful love story. Three hundred years ago there lived in India an emperor called Shah Jahan. His preferred wife was a beautiful and intelligent woman whom he loved greatly. Her title was Mumtazi Mahal, its shortened form, Taj Mahal, means 'pride of the palace'. In the year 1630 his beloved wife died. He decided to build her the most beautiful tomb that had ever been seen. It took more than 20,000 men working over a period of 18 years to build the Taj Mahal, indeed one of the most stunning buildings in the world.

FACT FILE

Minarets, or towers rise from each of the four corners of the Taj Mahal. The Taj itself soars another 200 feet into the air.

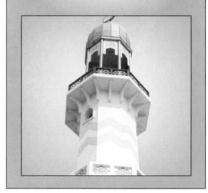

Francis Drake c.1541-1596

5p

Walter Raleigh c.1552-1618

7½p

WHEN WERE STAMPS FIRST USED?

It was in the sixteenth century that governments began to have regular postal services. They had three chief reasons for doing this. One was to enable them to inspect suspicious correspondence, the second was to produce revenue, and the third was to provide a service for the public. Henry VIII had a government postal service in England. In 1609, no one was allowed to carry letters except messengers authorized by the government. The whole system was finally changed in 1840. Stamps were introduced, and rates made uniform for all distances within the country, varying only according to the weight of the piece of mail. All other countries were to model their postal systems on that of Great Britain.

WHEN WERE THE SIGNS OF THE ZODIAC RECOGNIZED?

Capricorn

Recognition of the constellations can be traced to early civilizations. When people looked up at the sky at night they noticed that many of the brightest stars were arranged in a certain pattern or group. The part of the sky through which the sun, moon, and the planets travelled was named the Zodiac, meaning 'circle of living things'. The Zodiac was divided into twelve sections, each named after one of the twelve constellations. We know these constellations as Taurus, the bull; Aries, the ram; Pisces, the fish; Aquarius, the water carrier; Capricorn, the goat; Sagittarius, the archer; Scorpio, the scorpion; Libra, the scales; Virgo, the virgin; Leo, the lion; Cancer, the crab; and Gemini, the twins. The oldest record of the zodiacal signs as such is a wedge-shaped (or cuneiform) horoscope from 419 BCE.

Scorpio

Pisces

Libra, the scales

FACT FILE

In addition to the twelve constellations of the Zodiac, 36 other constellations were familiar to peoples of ancient times. These 48 are known as the 'ancient' constellations.

WHEN WAS THE SYDNEY OPERA HOUSE BUILT?

The Sydney Opera House in Australia is the busiest performing arts centre in the world. Construction of the building started in March 1959 and proceeded in slow stages over the next fourteen years. Since its opening in 1973, it has brought countless hours of entertainment to millions of people and has continued to attract the best in world class talent year after year. In an average year, the Sydney Opera House presents plays, musicals, opera, contemporary dance, ballet, every form of music from symphony concerts to jazz, as well as exhibitions and films.

FACT FILE

The original design of the Sydney Opera House called for two auditoriums. The government changed its mind and it was built with four, recently being updated to five.

WHEN DID BALLET BEGIN?

Ballet has been the dominant style in Western dance since its development as an independent form in the 17th century. Its characteristic style of movement is still based on the positions and steps developed in the court dances of the 16th and 17th centuries.

The most basic feature of the ballet style is the turned-out position of the legs and feet. The head is nearly always lifted and the arms are held out in extended curves. The body is nearly always held erect, apart from controlled arches in the back or a slight turning of the shoulders.

Ballet has, of course, undergone many stylistic alterations. The Romantic style of the early to mid-19th century was much softer – not involving so many jumps and turns – than the classical style of the late 19th and early 20th centuries. Russian ballet is often regarded as the model of the classical school, and is a mixture of various styles including the athleticism of Russian folk dances.

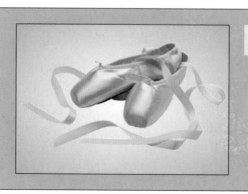

FACT FILE

Ballet dancers wear special shoes. These shoes have wooden blocks in the toes to enable the dancer to perform many of the complicated moves they make on the tips of their toes.

WHEN WERE BUTTONS FIRST USED?

Nobody really knows who first used buttons or when. They seem to go back to the beginning of history. Some experts say perhaps even 30,000 to 40,000 years ago! Yet in some parts of the world they have never been used at all. After all, there are so many different ways of fastening clothing to keep it in place: pinning, buckling, lacing, belting, wrapping around, or even tying together. In the fourteenth century buttons became popular in Europe and from that time on they have never gone entirely out of fashion. Buttons have been made from almost any kind of material you can imagine. Metals that buttons have been made of include gold, silver, steel, copper, tin, nickel, brass, pewter, and bronze.

FACT FILE

Animal products have also been used for making buttons and these include: bone, horn, hoof, hair, leather, ivory, and shells. The list is indeed endless, some have even been made from glass, paper and porcelain.

WHEN WERE CATS DOMESTICATED?

The cat has been around for a long, long time. Fossils of cats have been found which are millions of years old.

The domesticated cat we know today is the descendant of the wildcat, but just which wildcat we don't exactly know, because it happened too long ago. Probably the breeds of domesticated cats we know all came from two or three of the small wildcats that existed in Europe, North Africa, and Asia thousands of years ago. The most accurate answer to this question is that cats were domesticated around 5,000 years ago. Cats and humans spent about a thousand years establishing a close relationship, and eventually the cat proved to be a great companion and household pet.

FACT FILE

Egyptians worshipped the cat as a god. Their goddess Bast, or Pacht, was shown in pictures with a cat's head, and sacrifices were offered to cats. The cat represented their chief god and goddess, Ra and Isis.

WHEN WAS THE FIRST CARTOON DRAWN?

The word 'cartoon' was originally used by painters during the period of the Italian Renaissance. And in fact, it is still used today by artists. What they are referring to, however, is the first sketch in actual size of any work of art which covers a large area, such as a mural, a tapestry, or a stained-glass window.

When newspapers and magazines started to use drawings to illustrate news and provide amusement, these drawings also came to be called cartoons.

The first comic strips appeared in the early 1900s. Richard Outcault (the artist who created *Buster Brown*) published this comic strip in 1902. It was so popular that children all over the country wanted to dress in Buster Brown clothes. Another early comic strip was *Bringing Up Father*, which came out in 1912.

FACT FILE

In the days before newspapers, famous caricaturists like Hogarth, Goya, Daumier and Rowlandson made series of drawings on a single theme. These were the ancestors of the present-day cartoons and comic strips.

WHEN WAS THE FIRST COMIC BOOK MADE?

The *Yellow Kid* created by Richard Felton Outcault in 1895 is recognized as the first comic book.

Early forms of this sequential art can be seen in Paleolithic cave drawings, made by prehistoric man almost 20 thousand years ago.

The terms comics and comic strips became established around 1900 in the United States when all strips were indeed comic. Comic strips created from wood blocks date back to 1550.

A comic book is a bound collection of strips, typically telling a single story or a series of different stories. Most of the better newspaper strips eventually appear also in book form.

Before the advent of Superhero comic books there were Funny Books. People called them 'funny' books because inside were reprints of comic strips from newspapers, much like the *Garfield* or *Snoopy* strips you read today.

FACT FILE

Richard Felton Outcault was the first person to use the caption bubble or balloon, the space where what the characters say is written.

aaarghh!

WHEN DID THE EASTER EGG TRADITION BEGIN?

Many Easter customs go back to traditions that existed before Christianity itself. Both Easter and the coming of Spring are symbols of new life. The ancient Egyptians and Persians celebrated their Spring festivals by painting and eating eggs. This is because they considered the egg as a symbol of fertility and new life. The Christians also adopted the egg as symbolic of new life, the symbol of the Resurrection.

Another reason for the custom of giving eggs on Easter Sunday as a gift is because in the early days of the Church, eggs were forbidden food during Lent. With the ending of Lent, people were so glad to see and eat eggs again that they made it a tradition to eat them on Easter Sunday.

FACT FILE

In the legends of ancient Egypt, the rabbit is associated with the moon and became a symbol of a new period of life. The early Christians therefore used it too and linked it with Easter, the holiday that symbolizes new life.

WHEN WERE TOMBSTONES FIRST USED?

The use of tombstones and other grave-markers is common to many cultures and is an ancient practice first found in Africa.

The most impressive burial monuments are the great pyramids of ancient Egypt, which lie near Giza and were built in around 2500 BCE. In the late Stone Age and the early Bronze Age in parts of Europe, including southern Britain, people were buried in long and round barrows. Ancient Greek gravestones were decorated with sculptures, while Roman tombs had inscriptions and Hebrew graves were marked by pillars.

FACT FILE

It is thought that early man in Africa placed heavy stones on graves because they feared that evil spirits would rise from them. These, and other items, may also have marked graves as areas to avoid.

WHEN DO IGLOOS MELT?

A well-constructed igloo will last all winter, and only melt when the winter ends and the temperature rises to above freezing point, when the snow 'mortar' between the large snowblocks melts and the roof caves in. Two people can build a small igloo in a very short time, so they are convenient for journeys. Blocks of fresh snow are cut and shaped so that they slope inward when laid in circular courses. Each block is supported by those around it, making a very strong building. An entrance tunnel is added to one side and the hole at the top is filled with a large circular block. The gaps between the blocks are packed with more snow. Then a blubber lamp is lit and the tunnel is closed with a block of ice. The snow begins to soften and melt. When the door is re-opened, the sub-zero air rushes in, the blocks freeze into solid ice and the igloo becomes an immensely strong ice-house.

WHEN WAS THE FIRST LIGHTHOUSE BUILT?

The forerunners to the lighthouse were beacon fires kindled on hilltops, the earliest references to which are contained in the *Iliad* and the *Odyssey* (*c*. 8th century BCE). The first authenticated man-made lighthouse was the Pharos of Alexandria, which stood some 100 m (about 300 ft) high. The Romans erected many lighthouse towers in the course of expanding their empire, and by CE 400 there were some thirty in service from the Black Sea to the Atlantic. These included lighthouses at Boulogne, France and Dover, England. A fragment of the original Roman lighthouse at Dover still survives.

FACT FILE

Early lighthouses had wood fires or roches burning in the open, sometimes protected by a roof. After the 1st century BCE, candles or oil lamps were used in lanterns with panes of glass or horn.

WHEN WERE ORANGES FIRST BROUGHT TO AMERICA?

It was the Spaniards who were responsible for taking both the orange and the lemon to Florida and the West Indies. The first shipments were sent to New York and Philadelphia between 1880 and 1885. For the first time, a market for oranges was developed. Then orange orchards were set out in California, but on a smaller scale than in Florida.

Oranges are believed to be native to the tropical regions of Asia, especially the Malay Archipelago and, along with other citrus species, they have been cultivated from remote ages. Orange culture probably spread from its native habitat to India and the east coast of Africa and from there to the eastern Mediterranean region. The Roman conquests, the development of Arab trade routes, and the expansion of Islam, contributed greatly to their dispersal. By the time Christopher Columbus sailed, orange trees were common in the Canary Islands. Today oranges are cultivated in subtropical and tropical America, northern and eastern Mediterranean countries, Australia, and South Africa. Oranges thrive best where the trees are chilled somewhat by occasional light frosts in winter.

FACT FILE

Orange orchards are generally planted in relatively deep soil where drainage is good. They thrive in a wide range of soil conditions. The world production of oranges is approximately 70,000,000 metric tons annually.

WHEN DID PEOPLE START COOKING MEAT?

No one really knows how many thousands of years ago hunter-gatherers started cooking their food or how they learned that it was better that way. Before then, they would have had to eat everything they killed or gathered raw.

To begin with, meat would simply have been cut into chunks and roasted in the embers of a fire or on stones in a fire pit. Stones from the fire pit could also be thrown into water in a lined pit to boil food. Eventually, people learned to make fire- and waterproof pots, constructed of reed and clay, that could be placed on the fire or suspended over it .

FACT FILE

Cooking nowadays is done either by gas, oil or electricity on very modern stoves. The modern cook uses many different types of cooking pots, like the saucepan shown here.

WHEN IS REMEMBRANCE DAY?

Remembrance Day is an annual holiday on November 11th commemorating veterans of the armed forces and also the men and women killed in the country's wars. The observance originated as Armistice Day, which was set aside by the United States, Great Britain, and France to commemorate the ending of World War I (November 11, 1918). After World War II it was recognized as a day of tribute to the veterans and dead of that conflict as well. Poppies were in flower on many of the French battlefields of World War I. Today artificial poppies are sold in Europe and the USA to raise money for war veterans.

FACT FILE

World War I started with the assassination of the heir to the Austrian-Hungarian throne, Archduke Ferdinand, by a Serb patriot. Austria-Hungary, backed by Germany, retaliated against Serbia and the conflict began.

WHEN IS HALLOWE'EN?

Hallowe'en takes place on October 31st. Its name comes from All Hallows Eve, the day before All Hallows Day, now known as All Saints Day, on November 1st.

Traditional Hallowe'en customs may hold echoes of ancient autumn celebrations: the Druid festival of Samhain was when the souls of the wicked were gathered and this may have led to the superstition that they leave their graves on Hallowe'en, while the Roman goddess Pomona, wife of the god of autumn, Vortumnus, was worshipped by feasting around large bonfires on which autumn fruits were cooked.

FACT FILE

The Druid aspects of Hallowe'en probably developed into the link of witches and ghosts with this date and eventually developed into the modern American custom of 'trick or treat'.

WHEN WERE CHRISTMAS TREES FIRST INTRODUCED?

For families in North America, Germany, and other parts of Europe, the Christmas tree is the symbol of the Christmas season. Other evergreens have been a part of mid-winter festivals long before Christ. They played a symbolic part because they stayed green and alive when other plants appeared dead and bare. They represented everlasting life and hope for the return of spring. Primitive European tribes hung evergreens above their doors to offer the wandering winter spirits shelter within their homes, in the hope they would receive good fortune and health in return.

The use of evergreens and trees was and is most widespread in England and Germany. It can be traced back at least 500 years, when religious meaning began to be associated with these plants.

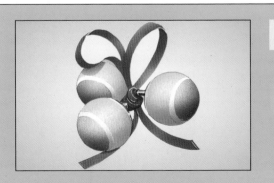

FACT FILE

It has now become traditional to decorate our Christmas trees with lights and ornaments as part of our festivities. The use of evergreen trees is an ancient custom of the Egyptians, Chinese and Hebrews.

WHEN WAS WALLPAPER FIRST USED?

Wallpaper developed soon after the introduction of papermaking to Europe, during the latter part of the 15th century. Although it is often assumed that the Chinese invented wallpaper, there is no evidence that it was in general use in Asia any earlier than the time of its appearance in Europe. The earliest wallpapers in England and France were hand painted or stencilled. During the 17th century, decorative techniques also included block printing and flocking, a process whereby powdered wool or metallic powders were scattered over paper on which a design had been drawn with a slow-drying adhesive. The oldest existing example of flocked wallpaper comes from Worcester and was created in approximately 1680.

FACT FILE

Wallpaper exists today of the designs of the artist William Morris (1834-1896). His style is very distinct and his work is much sought-after.

WHEN WAS THE INTERNAL COMBUSTION ENGINE DEVELOPED?

Though best known for his invention of the diesel engine, the French-born Rudolf Diesel was also an eminent thermal engineer, a connoisseur of the arts, a linguist, and a social theorist. During 1885 Diesel set up his first shop-laboratory in Paris and began his 13-year ordeal of creating his distinctive engine. At Augsburg, on August 10, 1893, Diesel's first model, a single 10-foot iron cylinder with a flywheel at its base, ran on its own power for the first time. Diesel spent two more years on improvements and on the last day of 1896 demonstrated another model with the spectacular mechanical efficiency of 75.6 percent. His engines were used to power pipelines, electric and water plants, automobiles and trucks and marine craft. It was also later used in applications including mines, oil fields, factories, and transoceanic shipping.

FACT FILE

Diesel originally conceived the combustion engine as an alternative to the oversized, expensive, fuel-wasting steam engine which was being widely used in industry.

WHEN WERE WEDDING RINGS FIRST WORN?

The wearing of a wedding ring is one of the oldest and most universal customs of mankind. The tradition goes back so far that no one can really tell how it first began.

The first people who actually used wedding rings in marriage were the Egyptians. In hieroglyphics, which is Egyptian picture-writing, a circle stands for eternity, and the wedding ring was a symbol of a marriage that would last forever. Christians began to use a ring in marriage around the year 900.

The fact that the ring is a circle may be one reason why it began to be used. The circle is a symbol of completeness. Some people believe that the wedding ring really started as a bracelet that was placed on women who were captured in primitive times. Gradually the circular bracelet on the arm or leg, which indicated that she was the property of one man in the tribe, was changed to a ring.

FACT FILE

The ring is worn on the fourth finger of the left hand because the ancient Greeks believed that a certain vein passed from this finger directly to the heart. The real reason, however, is that we use this finger least of all the fingers, so it is more convenient to wear an ornament on it.

WHEN DID WEDDINGS BEGIN?

Marriage, as a custom, goes back to the very earliest history of man. It has passed through three stages. The first was marriage by capture. Primitive man simply stole the woman he wanted for his wife.

Then came marriage by contract or purchase. A bride was bought by a man. Finally came the marriage based on mutual love. But even today we still have traces of the first two stages. 'Giving the bride away' is a relic of the time when the bride was really sold. The 'best man' at the weddings today probably goes back to the strong-armed warrior who helped primitive man carry off his captured bride. And the honeymoon itself symbolizes the period during which the bridegroom was forced to hide his captured bride until her kinsmen grew tired of searching for her.

Today we have weddings without realizing that this very word goes back to one of the early stages of marriage. Among the Anglo-Saxons, the 'wed' was the money, horses, or cattle which the groom gave as security for the purchase of his bride from her father.

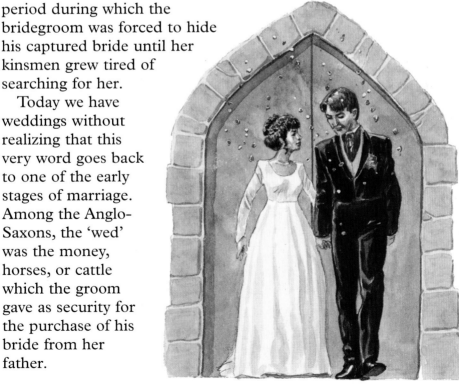

TELL ME WHEN : GENERAL KNOWLEDGE

WHEN WAS HONEY FIRST USED?

Honey is one of the most amazing products to be found in nature. It has been used since very ancient times, as it was practically the only way early man could get sugar. It was used originally as a medicine, to make a beverage called 'mead', and in a mixture with wine and other alcoholic drinks. In Egypt, it was used as an embalming material for their mummies.

In ancient India, it was used to preserve fruit and in the making of cakes and other foods. Honey is mentioned in the Bible, in the Koran, and in the writings of many ancient Greeks. So you can see its use goes far back into history.

There are hundreds of ways in which honey is used today. It adds sweetness to many foods such as fruits, candies and baked goods. It is used in ice cream, in medicines and for feeding babies. It is also given to athletes as a source of energy. Honey has been used in hand lotions, in antifreeze, and even as the centre (core) for golf balls.

FACT FILE

Honey bees are able to tell other colony members where good sources of food can be found by performing a special dance on their return to the hive.

WHEN DID BOXING BEGIN?

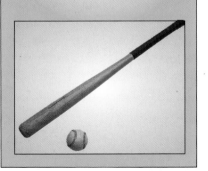

The first boxing bouts could be seen in ancient Greece, where the boxers performed at Olympic games and other public events. Some of the rules they observed were very much like the ones we have today. But there was one big difference – instead of gloves, the fighters wore *cestus*. This was a wrapping of leather studded with lead or bronze plates. One blow from a *cestus* could cause serious injury.

After the fall of the Roman Empire, boxing disappeared, not to reappear until it was revived in England at the beginning of the 18th century. It soon became a fashionable sport, and has remained so for more than 100 years.

WHEN WERE THE FIRST HOUSES BUILT?

People began to build homes, shelters for themselves and their families, thousands and thousands of years ago. The kinds of homes people built long ago depended almost completely upon the climate in which they lived, the building materials that were close at hand, and the dangers they faced in their daily lives.

The ancient Egyptians are believed to have been among the first to discover how to make bricks. In Mesopotamia primitive people later developed a way of making the sun-dried bricks harder and stronger. They placed the bricks in a hot fire and 'burned' them. Such bricks have lasted for thousands of years.

WHEN WAS FAST FOOD FIRST INTRODUCED?

Did you know there are more than 300,000 fast food restaurants in the United States? Fast food is so popular because it is convenient, predictable, and fast. Fast food has become a part of our busy lifestyles. But, nutrition experts point out, fast food is often high in calories, sodium, fat and cholesterol. This does not mean fast food is bad. But it does mean you should fit fast food into a balanced, healthy diet.

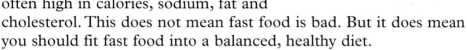

The sausage itself has been around since 900 bc; however, the hot dog was introduced during the Middle Ages, in Frankfurt-am-Main, Germany. A German butcher, Johann Geurghehner, developed a sausage that resembled a hound or hunting dog, which become known as the frankfurter or 'dachshund sausage'.

FACT FILE

In 1987 the city of Frankfurt celebrated the 500th birthday of the hot dog in that city. It is said that the frankfurter was developed there in 1484, five years before Christopher Columbus set sail for the new world.